CLASSIC CARS

DEDICATION

This book is dedicated to the memory of my grandparents, Lucy and Leicester Wagner.

ACKNOWLEDGMENTS

Many fantasies and myths are perpetuated in the automotive industry, and facts often become muddled in the storytelling. Whenever possible, facts in this book have been checked and double-checked. When in doubt, I consulted *Automobile Quarterly* as the final word. I wish to express my gratitude to Bill Snyder for contributing his expertise on most of the American marques. Special thanks go to Vince Manocchi, whose vast knowledge of classic cars goes beyond the vision of a photographer's eye. And warmest appreciation to my wife, Deniece Heredia-Wagner, for her deep well of patience while I was engaged in this project.

Contents

INTRODUCTION

When the Best Friend of Charleston pulled out of the railway yard at West Point Foundry in New York in 1830, it signaled the coming of the sometimes dirty, often uncomfortable business of transporting people from one place to another. Just one year later, the Best Friend was making regular runs between Charleston and Hamburg, South Carolina.

Transportation in the United States would never be the same.

Until the late nineteenth century, little thought was given to passengers of overland and transoceanic transportation. Spartan furnishings ruled the day. The object was to go from Point A to Point B as quickly as possible, regardless of comfort.

In the 1880s, when the railroads carried thousands of people from the East to Los Angeles, passengers roasted in the desert by day and froze by night. The seats were wooden, bathing was nonexistent, and the food was nothing more than low-quality meat slapped between two pieces of stale bread.

As these poor souls suffered to reach their land of opportunity, efforts to make travel more comfortable were under way. George Mortimer Pullman designed the sleeping car for the Chicago & Alton Railroad in 1858. He later created a larger and more elaborate sleeping car, which was used in Abraham Lincoln's funeral train from Washington, D.C., to Springfield, Illinois. In 1868, Pullman introduced the dining car, and the parlor car followed in 1875.

Efforts by designers like Pullman proved that transportation could be a comfortable if not luxurious experience. Perhaps the most famous—or infamous—example of luxury in ocean travel was the doomed Titanic, completed in 1912. As early as the 1880s, Karl Benz was thinking about comfort, evident in one of his early designs that featured an upholstered seat, a canopy, and gas-powered headlamps.

As America's roadways expanded in the second half of the nineteenth century, carriage builders began paying more attention to creature comforts. Europe, always leaps and bounds ahead of the United States in road improvements, already offered travelers some measure of comfort on the highway and the rails.

By 1908, Henry Ford had shaken up the burgeoning automotive industry with the introduction of the Model T and assembly-line production. Many people could now afford to own an automobile. Road improvements were slow to pick up, but the Tin Lizzy could navigate just about any road, trail, or pasture. By 1930, 700,000 miles (11,200km) of roads streaked across the country. The age of the automobile had finally arrived.

The classic car reigned between 1925 and 1948, during which time some of the finest examples of engineering and craftsmanship were married with stylish luxury. The argument could be made that the height of the classic car era was between 1925 and 1937, when automakers raced to outdo one another in engineering innovations while coach builders flourished before succumbing to the Depression and the public's condemnation of opulent living.

The portion of the classic car era preceding the fall of the stock market was also a period during which automotive marketing departments recognized the value of youth appeal. There were publicity advantages to having college-age men and women sporting around in Stutzes, Auburns, and LaSalles.

Although older, more established coach builders of the day abhorred the idea of unbridled youth careening down highways in their stately creations, younger designers, such as Harley Earl and Raymond Dietrich, reveled in designing cars that appealed to the young. Earl's LaSalle was the perfect vehicle for a wedding gift to a young couple or a college graduation present. Dietrich's Lincolns were particularly favored among young professionals who scoffed at the thought of buying a car like their parents' Packard or Pierce-Arrow when they could advertise their newfound station in society with panache.

Both Earl and Dietrich were firm believers that an automobile should be designed as a single unit. They broke away from the unspoken rule of the major coach builders of the day, whose only concern was the body from cowl to rear. These young men designed each model as a single unit with consistent themes in both the exterior and interior. The rear fenders, for example, carried the same design elements as the front fenders. Beltlines flowed easily from cowl to rear.

Earl and Dietrich, the young radicals of the era, shared the philosophy of such master coach builders as LeBaron Inc. and Brewster & Co. that the automobile's interior should be a place of comfort with a definite mood in which to travel. These coach builders took lessons from Pullman's sleeping and parlor cars and the floating palaces that sped across the Atlantic Ocean.

As a result, coach builders appropriated historical themes in the form of Georgian, Egyptian, Roman, and Renaissance motifs. Some creations were downright gaudy. Other, less grotesque designs were inspired by the world of nature, incorporating patterns based on birds, flowers, and leaves.

The period between 1925 and 1937 also reflected the industry's preoccupation with the research, development, and use of the multicylinder engine. A multicylinder engine is one that contains more than eight cylinders to power an automobile. It was as much a marketing gimmick ("more is better") as it was a real advance in technology.

Multicylinder engines allowed increased power to move these behemoths on the road, while still using a smaller cylinder size to provide smoother performance. Cadillac, with the financial backing of General Motors, reigned supreme in both technology and sales with its V16 engine, and was the only marque to make a profit from it. But in the late 1930s, advanced technology made multicylinder engines obsolete.

Another classic car concept was the streamlined design of a car. Chrysler's Airflow was not the first streamlined design to hit the market, but it certainly was the most radical when it debuted in 1934. It had followed the Cadillac AeroDynamic Coupe and Pierce Silver Arrow, which both debuted at the Chicago Century of Progress Exposition the previous year. The AeroDynamic Coupe had a drop-sided body with rounded window shapes and a very wide fastback that sloped dramatically to the rear bumper. The Silver Arrow featured a fastback body as well, but also had concealed running boards and its rear wheels concealed in full pontoon fenders. But the Chrysler's exterior was designed under air-current principles. It also moved the passenger area forward for a better ride and superior weight distribution.

The introductions of the Airflow, Cadillac's AeroDynamic Coupe, and the Silver Arrow were not happenstance. These automobile designs were born from one of the most significant events of the first half of the twentieth century: Charles A. Lindbergh's

Packard joined the multicylinder club relatively late compared to other luxury automakers, but its V12 was one of the best engineered engines in an American car. Unfortunately, it did little for Packard sales. Like many early 1930s Packards, the V12 Coupe body was adapted from the bodies originally manufactured for Eights.

historic transatlantic flight to France in 1927. Not only did automakers want to ride its publicity bandwagon, but they witnessed the significance of aerodynamics and streamlining in regard to performance and styling.

Offerings in this vein by Chrysler, Cadillac, and Pierce-Arrow never sat well with the buying public and were short-lived. But they laid the foundation for the development of body styles that exist today.

Ultimately, the Depression rendered useless the luxury automobile of the classic car era. Coach builders began falling like overage boxers as they continued to take great hits in their profit margins. But the lean economic times were only part of the demise of the great luxury car.

In a country that toyed with the idea of socialism before Franklin D. Roosevelt took office in 1933, there was little room for extravagant living. It was not considered tasteful to drive a moving palace powered by a V16 and trimmed in gold or silver with a Roman motif inside.

Modesty was the only appropriate avenue for the rich until the country weathered its economic storm. And with the coming of World War II and the subsequent postwar boom of mass-produced cars, cookie-cutter houses, and the single-minded goal of veterans to get a college education on the GI Bill, the day of the luxury car had outlived its usefulness.

Today, these cars remain a testament to early attempts at streamlining. And their beauty, which caused great excitement every year when new models were introduced, is unmatched to this day. It's no wonder that the preservation of these examples of rich and stylish living continues to thrive today through the work of professional restorers and private collectors.

Part One

United States

Auburn

WHILE MANY AUTOMOBILES OF THE CLASSIC CAR ERA ENJOYED UNPARALLELED SUCCESS IN ENGINEERING AND STYLING, THE Auburn was perhaps best known as one of the most unremarkable vehicles on the road, at least during the first two thirds of its thirty-six-year history. It was a very dependable, functional car that was promoted at one time by its makers as "The Satisfying Car," hardly the breathless enthusiasm the motoring public would expect from an automaker.

But long before Cord, Duesenberg, and Bugatti became household names, Auburn—more or less by trial and error—hammered away diligently year after year building a better car.

At Auburn's zenith in 1933, the Model 8-101 8-cylinder phaeton and the 12-161A 12-cylinder phaeton probably were responsible for enhancing Auburn's reputation as an automaker with body designs that needed little improvement.

The modest birth of the Auburn was the establishment of the Eckhart Carriage Company in Auburn, Indiana, in 1874. Civil War veteran Charles Eckhart was a wheelwright when he went to work for Studebaker, which was then building wagons and carriages in South Bend. Eckhart had a hankering to start his own business, and fortune smiled on him in 1866 when he married Barbara Ellen Ashleman, who had a large dowry. In 1874, the Eckharts sold their 80-acre (32ha) farm and bought a house and a 5-

OPPOSITE: Outrageous in design, this 1933 V12 Boattail Speedster was not the most practical car on the road. It seated only two people, who were forced to wrestle with the tiny convertible top. Perhaps most appealing was the very rakish windshield and unique boattail rear end. The Boattail Speedster won the American Stock Car Speed championships in 1932 and 1933 at speeds of up to 117 mph (187.2kph).

acre (2ha) plot of land in Auburn to start the Eckhart Carriage Company.

By 1893, Eckhart had retired and turned the business over to two of his sons, Frank and Morris. The Eckhart brothers grasped that automobiles were the future and were prepared to abandon the carriage business for the new invention. With $2,500, they founded the Auburn Automobile Company in 1900.

According to journalist Beverly Rae Kimes, the first car to come out of the struggling Eckhart brothers' plant was a tiller-steered single-cylinder runabout on solid tires, which sold for $800. They didn't sell many runabouts, and it was 1903 before they had something worthwhile to display at the Chicago Automobile Show. They still offered the runabout with chain drive, but they replaced the solid tires with pneumatic ones. In 1905, they came out with a 2-cylinder touring car, which they sold for more than $1,200. Four

years later, they produced a 4-cylinder version. In 1912, they graduated to a 6- cylinder engine.

Functional but not pretty, the Auburn vehicles enjoyed some success, particularly when the Eckhart brothers began offering optional accessories, such as headlights, windshields, and tops, as standard equipment. For the most part, this was the standard that Auburn lived by for the next two decades. If you bought an Auburn, you got a pretty good little car for the money. But then again, that could be said for many generations of cars. The Model T, the Studebaker Champion, the Falcon, and the Pinto all were dependable little cars, although not much distinguished them from the rest of the pack.

Auburn continued this trend in pre–World War I America, coming out with a 6-cylinder—Model 6-50—in 1912. Featuring a 41-horsepower Rutenber engine that sat on a 135-inch wheelbase,

the car sold for $3,000. In contrast, the 4-cylinder models ranged in price from $1,100 to $1,750, with up to 32 horsepower.

The Eckhart brothers bragged that they remained successful in the highly competitive automotive industry because ownership of their company had not changed, thereby ensuring stability. But in reality, their future did not look so bright. Sales were down, and in 1916 they attempted to provide variety to the customer with three different models that included three engines from different manufacturers: the Rutenber, Teetor, and Continental. But this strategy did not help sales. The carriage-production part of the business was discontinued in 1918, and one year later, a controlling interest in the Auburn was sold for about $1 million to a group of Chicago financiers, including chewing-gum magnate William Wrigley, Jr. Morris Eckhart was given a contract as president of the company.

Under the new ownership, the Auburn saw many changes, including the debut of the Auburn Beauty-SIX, a hint of things to come from Auburn. Produced in 1919, it was a handsome car with wind wings, front fender trunks on either side of the hood, and individual steps in place of running boards. This marked the first time that Auburn had focused on luxury items. The car was powered by a Continental 6-cylinder 25-horsepower Red Seal engine, but its performance could not match that of such cars as the Packard and Pierce-Arrow. Nevertheless, there were few complaints from buyers, probably because of the $2,000 bargain price.

Unfortunately, Auburn's timing was poor. A postwar depression hit the automaker hard. Only 15,717 units were sold over a four-year period. In 1924, Auburn was facing insolvency. It was producing only six cars a day, and even those could not be sold.

Enter E.L. Cord, who was handy at making money. In Chicago in 1919 with only $45 in his pocket, Cord got a job with the Quinlan Motor Company, which distributed Moon cars. Starting as a salesman, he quickly rose through the ranks, becoming general manager and ultimately purchasing an interest in the company. Now $100,000 richer and eager to invest his earnings, Cord set his sights on a vulnerable company with enormous potential—Auburn.

Cord was hired as general manager to revive the company; he also purchased a controlling interest. His first job was to sell the seven hundred Auburn touring cars that were sitting in the company parking lot. His predecessors may have seen a glass half empty, but Cord saw it half full. A little sprucing up of the inventory would get things moving, he believed. He immediately hauled the cars back into the plant and added nickel plating, repainted the bodies,

These Auburns on display at the 1912 Detroit Auto Show in no way heralded what was to come in the classic car era under E.L. Cord's leadership. Pedestrian and uninspired in styling, the Auburn was still a crackerjack under the hood with the debut in 1912 of its six-cylinder engine. These cars sat on a 135-inch wheelbase on thirty-seven-inch tires.

chopped the rooflines, and sold the entire lot for a half-million-dollar profit. Auburn paid off its debts, and Cord was promoted to vice president. In 1926, he became president.

Quality and understated elegance are admirable, but these characteristics do not necessarily translate into profits. Cord ensured that they would by instigating a vigorous sales campaign. He also streamlined the way Auburn conducted business.

Prior to Cord's arrival, there were very few Auburn showrooms in the country. Dealers were limited mostly to garage owners who owned one or two demonstration cars. Cord crisscrossed the country, talking to dealers and organizing a chain of showrooms. He also focused on export sales, establishing outlets in the Philippines, Australia, Germany, and Argentina. Export sales jumped nearly 100 percent between 1926 and 1928, and by 1928, Auburn had risen from fortieth place to eleventh in export sales.

Cord also brought in James Crawford as Auburn's new chief engineer. Crawford was to design a straight-eight, L-head, Lycoming engine (Cord later purchased the Lycoming company) to fit into the old 6-cylinder Auburn chassis.

This would become the 8-88 in early 1925, with a 276-cubic-inch engine that generated 60 braking horsepower at 2,850 rpm. The 8-88 featured a "twist-proof" frame, and a 3-speed "racing crash box" transmission. A second generation of the 8-88—now with a larger 299-cubic-inch, 68-horsepower engine—was manufactured in 1928 with hydraulic four-wheel brakes and a Bijur lubrication system.

Use of the Lycoming engine and Crawford's appearance on the scene were timely. The well-performing Mercer automobile had folded, and stock car racing was revived by the Contest Board of the American Automobile Association. Stutz, long a leader in early automotive racing, was left without a challenger. With Cord and Crawford, Auburn could fill the void.

According to journalist Beverly Rae Kimes, Cord sent his chief car tester, Wade Morton, to Los Angeles in March 1927 to put the 8-88 roadster on a 1,000-mile (1,600km) high-speed test run. Morton completed it in less than sixteen hours, for an average speed of 63.4 mph (101.4kph). In May, he drove in a 75-mile (120km) stock car race in Atlantic City against Stutz and Paige. Stutz nosed out Auburn for first place. But in that same year, Morton won first place at Rockingham Speedway in Salem, New Hampshire, averaging 89.9 mph (143.8kph). At the Pikes Peak Hill Climb and the 150-mile (240km) stock car race in Atlantic City, Auburn again finished second to Stutz.

Auburn, left, and Stutz were often fierce competitors on the race track. Competing in the 75-mile (120km) stock car race at the Atlantic City Speedway on May 7, 1927, the Auburn and Stutz finished only one-fifth of a second apart, with the Stutz winning by a nose.

Cord had nothing to be ashamed of. His Auburn roadster performed consistently, and its timings on the track were very close to those of Stutz.

Auburn's designs were so stylish that they were able to hold easily until 1930 without any significant changes. Sharply contrasting two-tone paint jobs emphasized the sweeping belt lines that ran up and over the hood to the radiator fill cap. The car's handsomely rakish windshield set the standard of automotive design for decades to come. And its flamboyant bobtail took the public by surprise.

While Cord chafed at Auburn's perennial second-place finishes to Stutz, these "defeats" did inspire him to build better machines. In 1928, he introduced the 8-115 model to replace the 8-88. This model kept the basic straight-eight 299-cubic-inch

Lycoming engine, but a two-barrel updraft carburetor boosted its horsepower to 115. This provided even more "oomph" than the Stutz, which had a 113-horsepower engine.

The new model featured a 130-inch wheelbase on a rigid 410-pound frame. The mechanical four-wheel brakes were replaced with hydraulic brakes.

The design was low-slung, very slender, and handsomely rakish. The 8-115 Speedster measured 180 inches long and a mere 56 inches tall, making the V-type windshield appear even more slanted. The belt line started high on the hood and tapered to a fine point in the rear. Bodies were manufactured by Limousine Body Company of Kalamazoo, Michigan. Auburn did not use traditional custom coach builders for its designs—it originally hired Murphy to design its convertible sedan, but later copied the design.

Finally, Cord had found his answer to the Stutz Blackhawk, although probably not quite to his satisfaction. In March 1928, Wade Morton hit the 108.46 mph (173.5kph) mark at Daytona. He also averaged 84.7 mph(135.5kph) in a twenty-four-hour period at Atlantic City.

Although Auburn could never quite match the romantic reputation of the Stutz, Cord had given his nemesis stiff competition and certainly had become part of the same elite class of stylish high-performance cars. Stutz was regarded as the faster of the two cars, but Auburn was just as pretty, almost as fast, and cost thousands of dollars less. The public flocked to Auburn showrooms, and the company's place in automotive history was secured.

More than 22,000 Auburns were sold in 1929, a 1,000 percent leap in sales since Cord had taken over the company five years earlier. Auburn's 6-cylinder cars averaged about $1,000, and the 8-cylinder models averaged between $1,400 and $2,150. A Stutz, by contrast, cost as much as $5,000.

Cord's only miscue came with his introduction in 1928 of the Cabin Speedster, an exotic machine with a paneled aluminum body on a 120-inch wheelbase and dropped frame. Its engine had 125 braking horsepower, and the styling was avant-garde. But the only model was destroyed in a fire at the 1929 Los Angeles Auto.

Despite this accident, the year 1929 would prove to be the best for Cord himself. He had already purchased Duesenberg Motors in Indianapolis as well as the Ansted Engine Company, Lexington Motor Car Company, and Central Manufacturing. He also founded the Cord Corporation and introduced the front-wheel-drive Cord L-29.

The stock market crash struck Auburn hard. Sales plummeted to 13,700 units in 1930, but rebounded nicely in 1931 with 28,103 cars sold, which met their recorded profits in 1929 before the crash.

By 1931, an estimated one thousand new Auburn dealers had joined the company, and the automaker jumped from twenty-third to thirteenth in retail sales. In 1932, Cord outdid himself by introducing a 12-cylinder engine that was the cheapest on the market.

This 392-cubic-inch engine developed 160 horsepower with dual carburetors, dual exhausts, and a Stromberg downdraft carburetor. With the V12, the light-bodied Auburn Speedsters reached speeds of 110 mph (176kph). Stripped of its fenders, the Speedster hit 118 mph (188.8kph). All this was packed into a no-frills car that sold for about $975 and that even required customers to pay extra for tires. Yet a fully equipped model still cost less than $2,000.

But the economic climate was changing, and Auburn began to flounder. Only 11,000 units were sold in 1932, and the figure dropped to a mere 6,000 by 1933.

In 1933, the number of models offered by the automaker was reduced from ten to seven. Prices were cut, and profits continued to slide. Auburn's ranking on the retailing market also took a nose-dive, from thirteenth place to twenty-first. The simple fact was that Cord was not giving his full attention to Auburn: he had too many other interests. He became involved in some business squabbles and left the United States for England in 1934 amid rumors of an SEC investigation.

Auburn attempted to stay afloat and produced one of its best cars to date—the Auburn 851 Speedster for 1935. This model proved to be Auburn's swan song. It came equipped with a straight-eight 115-horsepower Lycoming engine. The supercharged version by Kurt Beier, chief engineer of Schwitzer-Cummins, boosted the horsepower to a whopping 150 at 4,000 rpm.

Auburn could not afford to retool, so the radiator shell and hood design of the 851 were altered to change the basic lines. Teardrop fenders and a new tail were added to the 127-inch wheelbase. Designed by Gordon Buehrig, best known for his custom creations for Duesenberg, the 851 was a gorgeous car, although not much for comfort and space. There was little room for luggage, and only two people could fit inside. Moreover, two people were needed to remove or install the tiny convertible top. The standard raked split windshield, though, created the illusion of a very long car.

After taking over Auburn in 1924, E.L. Cord achieved his greatest sales success in 1929 with the 8-120. He sold more than 22,000 Auburns for a tenfold increase in sales. These 8-cylinder beauties ranged from $1,795 to $2,145.

The 1929 Speedster 8-120 differed little from the 8-115 of the previous year. It featured a 130-inch wheelbase on a very stiff and sturdy 410-pound frame that measured seven inches deep and three inches wide.

ABOVE: This Custom Phaeton sports a 12-cylinder, 341-cubic-inch engine that generates 100 horsepower, quite powerful in its day. The car sits on a 133-inch wheelbase and sold new for only $1,848.
OPPOSITE: This 1936 supercharged 852 Cabriolet was unchanged from the 851 offered the previous year. By 1936, Auburn was in deep financial trouble, and all it could afford was a name change. Between January and October 1936, only 4,830 Auburns were manufactured.

Four massive, flexible chrome exhaust pipes swept from the side hood panels.

The 851 could perform with the best. It easily exceeded 100 mph (160 kph), breaking seventy speed records in 1934. Only about five hundred 851 Speedsters were built in 1935 and 1936, and each sold for $2,245. Each sported a plaque on the dashboard with testers Wade Morton's or Ab Jenkins' signature on it. The plaque signified that the Speedster was tested at speeds of more than 100 mph (160kph). It is doubtful that Morton or Jenkins

actually tested each car, but the public was impressed, and gobbled the cars up anyway, according to *Automobile Quarterly*.

Auburn's sales were up by 20 percent, but the company lost a good deal of money on each car because each 851 Speedster was virtually hand-built. Although the 851 Speedster still drew customers into the showroom, they usually left not with an 851, but with cheaper 6- and 8-cylinder models.

Auburn had toyed with the idea of a diesel-powered nine-passenger airport limousine, but the idea quickly died. Instead, the

Auburn 852 debuted in 1936, and it differed little from the 851. Gordon Buehrig sarcastically described the new model as "our facelift for that year."

Only 4,830 cars were produced by Auburn during a ten-month period in 1936. It offered no automobiles in 1937.

Cord returned to the United States in 1936, but the honeymoon he had enjoyed for more than ten years was long over. Although he left Auburn an unpopular man, few people today would remember the marque if Cord had not assumed control.

Cadillac

Unlike Auburn, Cadillac never concerned itself with developing a high-performance car, although its V16 models could easily top 90 mph (144kph). Instead, Cadillac was primarily concerned with styling to attract the older, wealthier clientele of the 1920s and 1930s. Throughout the 1920s, it steadily gained its niche in the market, but Packard still set the standard in luxury. It seemed that Cadillac was always one step behind its rival, yet it was Cadillac that survived the Depression and ultimately set the standard in the luxury car field, leaving an economically battered Packard to limp through the 1940s and 1950s.

Cadillac, however, was in a precarious position in 1930 following the crash of the stock market—it was struggling along with everyone else. Many independent marques died during this time, and Cadillac—if it had been an independent—would have followed them to the grave. Cadillac averaged about 20,000 cars annually, reaching its zenith in 1928 with 41,000 cars sold. But the crash served as a wake-up call when sales fell dramatically. Faced with its impending

OPPOSITE: This rare right-hand drive 1931 V16 Cadillac Phaeton embodies the perfect combination of elan and performance. While it couldn't quite match the speeds of a Duesenberg, it reigned in smoothness and quiet performance. The best of the multicylinder cars, it had 16 cylinders with a 3×4 bore and stroke, displacing 452 cubic inches. The spark plug and ignition wiring were hidden under a shroud inside the 45-degree V in the engine.
ABOVE: Cadillac's famed mascot on a 1931 V16 Town Car

demise, Cadillac was forced to reevaluate its market.

There were many survivors of the Depression who could easily afford a Cadillac, certainly enough to keep the division of General Motors solvent. But buyers, nervous about flaunting their wealth in a luxury car, knew that it was almost socially unacceptable to drive anything with more than 8 cylinders.

Auburn and Cord had an excuse: their image was tied to high-performance driving. Cadillac bespoke only affluence and might as well have had tattooed on the owner's forehead, "I'm wealthy."

As a result, Cadillac began building more modest cars, concentrating on 8-cylinder models. It still built a small number of ultra-luxury cars, thanks to the support of General Motors, but modesty ruled the day. Packard virtually abandoned its blue-chip image during this period, when it introduced the modestly priced Packard 120, allowing Cadillac to grab some of the luxury market.

Cadillac was not originally created as a luxury car, but as a moderately priced runabout that sold for about $750. But what set Cadillac apart from other marques was its attractive looks. While virtually every automobile manufactured at the turn of the century had the look of a rough-hewn horse buggy that happened to be powered by a gasoline engine, the Cadillac had the refined image of a diamond: it was a very pretty vehicle.

Henry Leland was fifty-nine years old when he helped found the Cadillac Automobile Company in Detroit with moneymen William Murphy and Lemuel W. Bowen and engineer Robert C. Faulconer. Named after the French founder of Detroit, Antoine de la Mothe Cadillac, the runabout was perhaps the first Detroit automobile to be recognized for styling rather than performance.

But Leland never ignored the engineering side of automobile manufacturing. As a young man, he learned precision manufacturing from both Samuel Colt in Connecticut and the Brown & Sharpe precision machine shop, which provided the foundation for precision machining that would become the hallmark of Cadillac. While taken for granted today, precision machined parts were advanced technology in the late nineteenth century. It was Leland's insistence

This car was initially named the Runabout by its creator, Henry Martyns Leland, but Cadillac publications later identified this 1903 vehicle as the Model A. The single-cylinder horizontal engine was located under the front seat. This model is clearly preparing for a race, given the noticeable absence of lights and top.

on precision manufacturing that would later make his cars the most desirable products of the General Motors line.

By 1890, Leland had moved his family to Detroit, which was at the time experiencing its phenomenal growth in machining. Joining Faulconer, he began manufacturing steam engines for streetcars and gasoline units for boats. He quickly attracted the attention of Ransom Eli Olds, owner of the Olds Motor Works, who was seeking a new engine for his curved dash automobiles. Leland won a contract to build 2,000 motors. He developed an engine that provided 23 percent more horsepower than the current version used in Oldsmobile. But Olds rejected it as too costly.

In 1902, Murphy and Bowen approached Leland to evaluate their own automobile plant in an effort to sell it. Murphy and Bowen had been associated with Henry Ford, but had become frustrated with the legendary automaker's preoccupation with racing cars instead of paying more attention to designing and manufacturing them for the public.

Leland saw an opportunity to market his new engine. He talked the two men into keeping their plant open, and Cadillac was born. The firm of Leland & Faulconer manufactured the engines and drive lines, and the Cadillac Automobile Company built the

bodies and frames. In October 1902, the Model A Cadillac rolled out of the plant.

The marque was an immediate success. More than 2,200 orders were taken at the January 1903 New York Automobile Show. The little runabout featured a 10-horsepower, single-cylinder, copper-jacketed engine with a 2-speed planetary transmission. Reliable and state-of-the art for its time, the car also had refinement and style, something entirely new for 1903.

Between 1903 and 1908, more than 16,000 cars were sold. The automaker hit a milestone in 1908 when it won the prestigious Royal Automobile Club's Dewar Trophy for the most important automotive advanced technology. The trophy recognized Leland's most pressing concern: precision.

Leland had three of his cars race at the Brooklands track in England, then had each dismantled completely. The parts were thrown into a single pile, then reassembled into three new Cadillacs with no machining permitted. The three cars were built with the interchangeable parts, and each ran as perfectly as the three vehicles before disassembly.

Cadillac's reputation had grown so fast that it attracted the attention of William C. Durant. In July 1909, Durant acquired Cadillac for $5.6 million. Cadillac joined Olds, Oakland, and Buick under a single umbrella to form General Motors. GM was reorganized in 1916, and Leland and his son, Wilfred, were given unprecedented power to remain an independent operation.

Cadillac began building 4-cylinder models in 1905 and came to produce about 75,000 units by 1914. Instead of developing a 6-cylinder engine like that of its competitors, Cadillac shocked the industry by jumping to a 70-horsepower V8 in 1914. The V8 would remain the basic template for all Cadillac power plants. It would also create a legion of imitators, including Peerless, Daniels, Cole, and Cunningham.

Cadillac did well during this period, but the Lelands' days were numbered. William Durant fired the father and son, reportedly because their egos grew too big for the division. Another story, and probably a more accurate one, was that Durant refused to produce Liberty aircraft engines for the war effort, so the Lelands resigned and established the Lincoln Motor Company to build the engines.

This 1929 341-B is very similar to the 1928 341-A. But Cadillac dressed up the 1929 version by chrome-plating all the brightwork and moving the side lights to the fenders. In addition, the 341-B received Security-Plate safety glass and electric windshield wipers. The 341-B sold for about $3,600.

Durant later changed his mind, but by that time father and son had already left. Cadillac management then fell into chaos.

Richard H. Collins, formerly associated with Buick, became general manager of Cadillac, but left in 1921 for Peerless and took his chief engineer with him. Herbert H. Rice replaced Collins but did nothing remarkable for Cadillac and departed in 1925.

Cadillac's outlook brightened when Lawrence P. Fisher, Jr., assumed the presidency that year. For the next decade, the GM division witnessed rapid growth.

Fisher was one of seven brothers, two of whom founded the Fisher Body Company in 1908. Fisher Body regularly made coaches for Cadillac and Buick, so it was no surprise when General Motors purchased a controlling interest in the company in 1919. By 1925, Fisher had purchased Fleetwood, a Pennsylvania-based coach-building firm.

As Cadillac settled down to business after the departure of the Lelands, it began to upgrade the basic V8 engine that Henry Leland had pioneered in 1914. In September 1927, the V8 had become a compact, rigid 341-cubic-inch engine that boosted the horsepower to 95. This basic engine would serve Cadillac well for more than two decades, but many other automobiles on the road—among them Auburn and Stutz—had far bigger engines.

Cadillac had a number of engineering innovations. Ernest Seaholm, who came on board in 1923 and remained for twenty years, was largely responsible for the numerous changes. He developed the synchronized-shifting transmission and four-wheel brakes. In 1932, he developed Vacuum-servo assisted brakes for the larger models, and in 1937 he was instrumental in helping the division convert to hydraulic brakes.

The gains that the automaker made in engineering were diminished by lazy styling. Stylish designs remained a novelty in the mid-1920s, and were primarily reserved for the young nouveau riche. By contrast, Cadillac projected staid conservatism, which suited older, wealthy buyers just fine.

But Fisher knew that to stay competitive, he had to provide the public with innovative designs. He found his answer in Harley Earl, a graduate of Stanford University and the son of a coach builder. Fisher discovered Earl while touring Cadillac dealerships in 1925. The young man used modeling clay to experiment with shapes and surfaces, and he designed each car as an entire unit rather than as a mere piece of coachwork. Fisher eagerly brought Earl back to Detroit from Los Angeles, and Earl in turn promptly developed the LaSalle, the first pocket luxury car with a 125-inch wheelbase to debut on the market. It was smaller and less expensive than the full-sized line, and was produced to extend Cadillac's prestige line.

Earl wanted to build not only a well-engineered car, but one that reflected the social position of its owners. Many Cadillac models of the late twenties and early thirties hinted strongly of Hispano-Suiza influences. The 1929 Cadillac Series 341-B Fleetwood town car—and other high-end Cadillacs of the period—had a feminine touch that delighted buyers in the luxury market. The Series 341-B featured lacy wire wheels, rakishly cut front fenders, scalloped hoods, a delicately designed radiator, and ribbed headlight shells.

In 1928 and 1929, the marque featured its lavish "Nature's Studios" interiors. GM president Alfred P. Sloan, for example, had his limousine equipped with reading lamps with exposed bulbs and reflectors, a frosted urn design cut into a vanity mirror, a wood-ribbed headliner, and inlaid smoking sets.

These features erased any doubts that Cadillac was part of the classic car class. Its reputation was further enhanced in 1930 with the debut of the 452-cubic-inch, 165-horsepower V16 engine and the 370-cubic-inch, 135-horsepower V12. Four years later, the V16 would be boosted to 185 horsepower and the V12 to 150.

The V16 and V12, coupled with Ernest Seaholm's SynchroMesh 3-speed transmission, which eliminated the need for double clutching, provided a much smoother ride and outperformed all competitors except Duesenberg. The problem for Cadillac, however, remained Packard. The independent was firmly entrenched in the luxury car market, and the Packard Eight still provided a smoother and faster ride than the Cadillac. Fisher saw his edge with the V16 and V12.

The V16 featured a bank of eight cylinders on each side of the block and mounted in a V form. It was placed on a common crankcase and drove a common crankshaft. Each bank of cylinders had its own manifold, water pump, ignition circuit, and carburetor. The car could actually run on a single bank of cylinders.

Aesthetically, the bodies of the V16 did not look much different from those of the V8 models. Designed by Harley Earl and built by Fleetwood, the V16 bodies had a special curved molding added to the hood so that buyers could tell the difference between the two versions. Christened the "Madame X," the V16 featured a V-shaped windshield. A bar crossed the radiator and carried a big "V" with "16" splashed across it. The V16 was mounted on a 148-inch wheelbase, and the V12 was placed on a 140-inch wheelbase, the same as the 8-cylinder models.

Perhaps the best example of the V16 is the dual cowl phaeton. This car reigned supreme in the luxury car market during 1930 and 1931.

The V16 dual cowl phaeton is not to be confused with Fleetwood's 4260 sport phaeton. Only 85 sport phaetons were manufactured. Many owners had them converted to dual cowls by independent coach builders. Only a handful of original dual cowl phaetons were manufactured at the Fleetwood plant. In fact, *Automobile Quarterly* reported in 1985 that perhaps as few as three dual cowl phaetons were shipped by Fleetwood. One was transported to Ohio and two to San Francisco. Documents for one model shipped to San Francisco listed a "double cowl" as an option for the phaeton. This phaeton, according to *Automobile Quarterly*, featured a classic swing-up rear cowling and an unusual hinged rear windshield.

Prices for Cadillacs ranged from $3,295 for a V8 coupe to as much as $10,000 for the V16 town brougham. In all, eleven body styles were available for the V8 chassis, twenty-one bodies for the V12 models, and thirty different styles for the V16. The Series 452-A offered fifty-four Fleetwood body styles.

By 1932, significant changes had been made in the body styles. The light touch of the Hispano-Suiza was abandoned in favor of an art moderne motif. This design was decidedly more masculine, with rugged four-tiered tubular bumpers, concentric-cone horn trumpets, and horizontal hood and fender louvers. Even the delicate goddess radiator mascot with backstretched arms and windblown gown became less fragile in appearance. Inexplicably, she was redesigned to be heavier and stronger, with wings that did not signal windswept freedom on the highways, but rather a "get-out-of-my-way" glare.

OPPOSITE: Perhaps the ultimate in chic when it comes to open-car driving, the 1930 V16 sport phaeton had a short rear cowling in front of the rear passenger seat, which housed a roll-up windshield. Eighty-five such bodies were produced by coach builder Fleetwood.

CLASSIC CARS

ROB L. WAGNER

MetroBooks

MetroBooks

An Imprint of Friedman/Fairfax Publishers

Library of Congress Cataloging-in-Publication Data

Wagner, Rob L., date
   Classic cars / by Rob L. Wagner.
      p.   cm.
   Includes index.
   ISBN 1-56799-286-2 (HC)
   1. Automobiles—History. 2. Automobiles—Collectors and
collecting. I. Title.
TL15.W274   1996
629.222—dc20   95-52715
                CIP

Editor: Tony Burgess
Art Director: Jeff Batzli
Designer: Kevin Ullrich
Photography Editor: Emilya Naymark

Color separations by Ocean Graphic International Company Ltd..
Printed in China by Leefung-Asco Printers Ltd.

For bulk purchases and special sales, please contact:
Friedman / Fairfax Publishers
Attention: Sales Department
15 West 26th Street
New York, NY 10010
212/685-6610 FAX 212/685-1307

ABOVE: The introduction of the 452-B in 1932 marked a pull-back by Cadillac in size and quality, as its dominance in multicylinder cars was challenged by other automakers and as the Depression took a stranglehold on the U.S. economy. This Cadillac features modest hardware and exterior trim and less flashy coachwork. OPPOSITE TOP: The year 1933 produced many styling firsts for automakers, and Cadillac was the king of the hill in design. Cadillac abandoned the traditional square-rigged styling for the more streamlined form that came to typify the classic car era. This 1933 V16 Fleetwood convertible sedan is a prime example of the art moderne motif, with horizontal hood and fender louvers, conical horn trumpets, and finned hubcaps. OPPOSITE BOTTOM: A 1934 LaSalle convertible. With the introduction of the LaSalle, Cadillac abandoned the pocket luxury market. The 1934 model year saw the LaSalle become a medium-priced offering on a 120-inch wheelbase powered by a 240-cubic-inch Oldsmobile straight-eight engine.

These cars sold in very limited numbers during 1930 and 1931, but did fairly well overall for the decade. Only 3,250 V16s and 5,725 V12s were manufactured in 1930 and 1931. Unique, if not brazen, in engineering, the V16 and V12 engines held no real practical use. Advanced technology later in the decade made these engines obsolete. Precision-insert connecting rod bearings helped eliminate knock and high-speed wear on any engine with fewer than 12 cylinders. Driving a V16, the driver was lucky to get 8 miles (12.8km) to a gallon of gasoline and 150 miles (240km) to a quart of oil. Yet the 16s and 12s did garner loyalty, with 15,207 produced through 1938, when both engines were discontinued. They were replaced with the flathead 185-horsepower version of the V16.

Although the larger engines created a sensation among automotive writers of the era, the V8 models had always been Cadillac's bread-and-butter cars. With a keen sense of what the public wanted in Depression-era America, Cadillac concentrated on marketing the V8s. It managed to build 10,000 V8 models in 1930 and 1931, then suffered along with all the other makers in 1932 and 1933, with only about 3,000 cars made. But from 1934 until World War II, Cadillac produced an increasing number of cars, with annual sales peaking in 1939 at about 13,000 units.

Lawrence Fisher was transferred to another assignment in 1934, and Cadillac found a new chief in Nicholas Dreystadt, who cut costs by streamlining operations. It was a necessary step that worked, as Cadillac still produced luxury cars at competitive prices. Dreystadt's most significant move was in 1934, when he moved LaSalle further into a medium-priced range. LaSalle's wheelbase was shortened to 120 inches, and the V8 was replaced with an Oldsmobile 240-cubic-inch straight-eight. The move caused LaSalle to abandon the luxury car market, but it was still a good year ahead of the Packard 120 in reaching buyers with limited spending money.

Like Fisher, Dreystadt insisted on new styling and engineering innovations. A steering column–mounted gearshift was introduced in 1938, and Bill Mitchell, a young protégé of Harley Earl, developed the V8 Sixty Special that featured the then-dramatic notched back and no running boards. By eliminating the running boards, Cadillac was able to provide a wider interior.

By the end of the decade, Cadillac was a leader of the prestige car market, surpassing Chrysler and Packard and surviving such trendsetters as Duesenberg and Cord. The integrity of the marque begun by Henry Leland and Lawrence Fisher remained uncompromised as it entered the postwar era.

Cord

ERRETT LOBBAN CORD HAD HIS HANDS FULL IN **1929**, JUGGLING A NUMBER OF EMPIRES, including Duesenberg, Auburn, and Cord. His Auburns had proven a modest success on the market, and the Duesenberg would become the symbol of unbridled Roaring Twenties flashiness. Cord wanted something between the reasonably priced Auburn and the extravagant Duesenberg—a new automobile featuring advanced technology and radical styling that would be a standard for decades to come.

His proposed L-29 project had evolved into a front-wheel-drive Cord with a very low silhouette. Front-wheel drive in 1929 was clearly a work-in-progress venture. (Actually, two front-wheel drives were introduced in 1929, with Cord beating Archie Andrews' Ruxton by a few months.) Cord helped pioneer the technology, but the Cord L-29 had earned a bad reputation by the 1950s, when parts were wearing out and had become difficult to replace.

OPPOSITE: The Cord 810/812 design by Gordon Buehrig was named in 1949 as one of the ten best designs at the Museum of Modern Art in New York City. This 1937 Cord 812 convertible was chock-full of innovations. Its front-wheel drive allowed for a lower silhouette. It provided a step-down floor instead of running boards, and the headlights retracted into the fenders. ABOVE: Like the 810, this 812 rectangular panel on the dashboard is a dramatic departure from other classic era cars. Consisting of components from surplus stock, the calibrated gauges were either round or fanned and grouped close together for easy eye access. A pair of glove boxes flanked the panel, and the speaker for the optional radio was mounted above the windshield.

E. L. Cord had contributed some of the problems associated with the L-29. He wanted a front-wheel-drive car for aesthetics and marketing potential, not as an engineering innovation. A car with a low silhouette was undeniably attractive, but engineers were skeptical that front-wheel drive could work on a heavy luxury car.

Designed by race car engineers Harry Miller and Cornelius Van Ranst, the first Cord prototype was completed in late 1928. The two engineers immediately took E. L. Cord for a drive around Beverly Hills. Cord gushed over the auto's performance, but Miller and Van Ranst were less than enthusiastic. The noise level of the drivetrain at low speeds was horrible, and the steering vibrated a lot on uphill turns. The pair wanted to correct these deficiencies and work out other problems. But Cord would have none of it. He wanted four more prototypes in January 1929, with production beginning in August at the Auburn, Indiana, plant.

The L-29 offered distinct advantages, primarily the absence of the driveshaft, which created a lower center of gravity and the elimination of the high tunnel through the center of the interior of the automobile. The low center of gravity also contributed to the stability of high-speed cornering.

Yet the L-29 did poorly on hills. Because of its long straight-eight engine and unusual gearbox/differential placement due to the front-wheel drive and 137.5-inch wheelbase, most of the weight was on the rear of the car. This made traction poor on the front wheels. It was not until the Model 810 debuted in 1936 that the center of weight was moved forward to improve performance.

The L-29 was powered by a 299-cubic-inch, 125-horsepower Lycoming L-head eight engine, the same power plant supplied to Cord's Model 125 Auburn. The engine was reversed—the front placed next to the firewall—with the clutch, transmission, and differential housing bolted together as a single unit. One bizarre feature of the L-29 was the 7-foot (2.1m) shift lever that passed over the engine to reach the driver.

In addition to the less-than-desirable front-wheel drive was the irksome transmission. Shifting from one gear to another was clunky, which tended to erode the opinion that the L-29 was a sports car. And what made matters worse, it took a little more than thirty seconds for the car to go from 0 to 60 mph (0 to 96kph). Its top speed, however, was about 85 mph (136kph), which was comparable to other performance cars of the day.

Whatever mechanical shortcomings the L-29 suffered, its sensational styling helped keep it in the public eye. Its low silhouette (the car stood only 61 inches tall) and long flowing hood gave

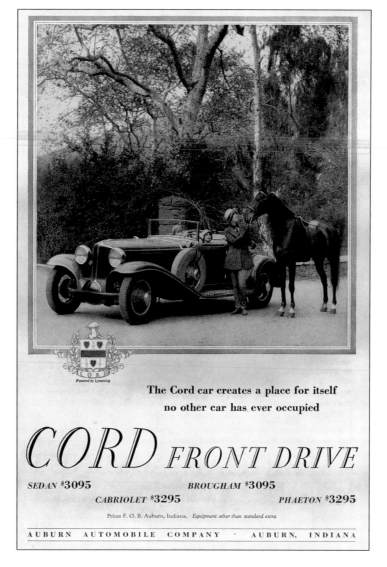

The Cord car creates a place for itself
no other car has ever occupied

CORD FRONT DRIVE

SEDAN $3095   BROUGHAM $3095
CABRIOLET $3295   PHAETON $3295

Prices F. O. B. Auburn, Indiana. Equipment other than standard extra

AUBURN AUTOMOBILE COMPANY · AUBURN, INDIANA

OPPOSITE: America's first front-wheel-drive car, the L-29, was a visual masterpiece that was reputedly beset with chronic mechanical problems. Cord enthusiasts today may argue that point, citing the fact that complaints arose mostly in the 1950s, when parts were no longer available. ABOVE: E. L. Cord chose the worst possible moment to introduce his front-wheel drive L-29. With the stock market crash just weeks away, advertisements like this one sought to place the L-29 at the top of the luxury market.

the illusion of larger proportions. It was undeniably attractive. Taken as a whole, there was nothing revolutionary about the car's design. Some styling, like the V radiator grille, was introduced on the Duesenberg J the year before the L-29 hit the market (Duesenberg's designers also styled the L-29). What made the L-29 stand apart from its competitors was its dramatic low body, dipped belt line, and roof design. Cord eschewed adornments, preferring traditional forms. The L-29 garnered several awards in the European Concours d'Elegance, and many of its features were pirated by other automakers.

Prices for the L-29 ranged from $3,095 to $3,294 for the convertible cabriolet, sedan, phaeton, and brougham. It was expensive for its day, but considerably cheaper than other specialty models like Stutz, Lincoln, Packard, and Marmon.

Cord's timing to introduce the L-29 could not have been worse. Debuting two months before the October 1929 stock market crash, the L-29 never had a chance to sell well. By 1931, Cord had slashed prices on all models by $800, but that did not help. During the L-29's entire run through 1932, only 4,429 were sold.

Every luxury car on the market was suffering from poor sales, but the L-29 could never overcome the Depression. It did well on the open road, as long as that road was flat. But it handled poorly in parking and low-speed driving. And its front-wheel drive gave it the temperament of a European sports car, requiring frequent visits to the repair shop.

While characterized as a pathetic failure in its day, the L-29 is considered a classic because of its innovations, especially the front-wheel-drive option that is common on today's vehicles.

It also served as a precursor to Cord's Models 810 and 812, which were introduced in 1936 and 1937, respectively.

But the Cord empire had been crumbling. He sought an automobile that would stop his competitors dead in their tracks. He came up with the Model 810—and later the 812—designed by Gordon Buehrig.

In 1933, Buehrig started developing the 810, which had originally been intended as a medium-priced Duesenberg on an Auburn chassis. But six months later, it ended up as a front-wheel-drive Cord. Cord probably had only $1 million in resources in his Auburn-Cord-Duesenberg empire. He had to make do by resurrecting his front-wheel-drive version with a radical design.

The project took nearly a year to get off the ground as Cord officials debated whether they wanted the Duesenberg or a new Cord. In the summer of 1935, they began building the 810.

This "coffin-nose" beauty with wraparound venetian-blind radiator louvers, pontoon-style fenders, and exposed exhaust pipes (introduced in 1937) was full of firsts. It featured hand-operated concealed headlights, dual taillights with a separate license plate light, a roof-mounted radio speaker, a hidden gasoline cap, and full wheel covers. (All these innovations came to be routinely used on most postwar automobiles.) The car was also free of running boards and had a step-down floor, long before Hudson touted its step-down versions in the late 1940s.

Most of the gauges on the automobile's instrument panel were closely clustered. Cord attempted to break away from the Detroit crowd to provide a full complement of round or fanned gauges to aid the operator. Instruments on a rectangular panel measured the speed, oil pressure, water, gasoline, oil quantity, rpm, and electric charge. Toggle switches were placed in a central housing at the bottom of the panel, and large knobs in the upper corners of the panel opened the windshield panes for ventilation on the enclosed models. Glove boxes were located at each end of the dashboard.

The 810 was equipped with a 289-cubic-inch Lycoming V8 that produced 125 braking horsepower at 3,500 rpm. The addition of the Schwitzer-Cummins centrifugal supercharger on later models produced 170 braking horsepower at 4,200 rpm that could top 110 mph (176kph) and go from 0 to 60 mph (0 to 96kph) in thirteen seconds.

Both the 810 and 812 came on a 125-inch wheelbase. They were offered in four body styles: phaeton, sportsman convertible, Westchester sedan, and Beverly sedan. The 812 also came in the custom Beverly models. The Westchester and Beverly featured a two-window fastback sedan body. The Beverly had piped broad-cloth upholstery and a permanent dividing armrest on some models in the rear seat to distinguish it from the Westchester. These automobiles ranged in price from $1,995 to $3,060.

The 810 and 812 today are instantly recognized as Cords and are the perfect examples of the specialty merchandise field in the automotive industry. But getting the 810 on the market was not without problems. Typical of Cords, the 810 was beset with mechanical problems. These setbacks could have been solved if engineers had had the opportunity to perfect the car, but there was no time for thorough testing. Cord was determined to have one hundred cars ready for the November 1935 New York show. Officials at the show did not want to see "one-off" prototypes, so Cord and Buehrig had to manufacture one hundred models in less than five months. Buehrig was compelled to have each car hand-

OPPOSITE: Following a four-year absence, Cord returned with the 1936 Cord 810. It was a dramatic departure from the L-29, but it retained the Cord concept of originality and radical design. Dubbed the "coffin-nose" because of its long hood and vertical louvers, the car sat on a 125-inch wheelbase and was powered by a 289-cubic-inch V8 engines. Note the supercharger hoses on the Sportsman Coupe. ABOVE: Designed by Philip Wright, who had worked for coach builder Murphy of Pasadena, California, the Cord Speedster was even more radical than the L-29 with its sweeping two-tone paint scheme, pontoon fenders, and lack of running boards. This Speedster is a replica built on an original Cord chassis. The original was destroyed.

built. He finished all one hundred, but they arrived at the show without transmissions.

It didn't matter. The 810s were wildly popular with the public. A show survey rated the Cord the best-looking car on display, with the Packard 120 taking second place. Orders poured in, and Cord officials promised deliveries by Christmas. But Christmas came and went, and no Cord 810s were delivered. Buehrig was still trying to correct overheating and transmission flaws. By the time the problems were solved, Cord had lost its momentum and enthusiasm had dwindled.

Sales were so low that fewer than one hundred cars were produced each month. In all, only a thousand 810s were produced

before the 812s replaced them in November 1936. The biggest difference between the two models was a $415 optional supercharger available on the 812. The 812 fared better than its sister model, with slightly more than 1,300 units sold. In all, 2,320 810s and 812s were manufactured. Today, more than 50 percent of the 810s and 812s manufactured are still in existence.

E. L. Cord's automobile concerns collapsed in 1937. Continued economic hardships during the Depression and unorthodox styling doomed the L-29, 810, and 812 from the start. Auburn and Duesenberg had already ceased production. The sickly survivor, the Cord 812, died an inglorious death on August 7, 1937, when the last of the 812s rolled off the assembly line.

Duesenberg

At its peak, Duesenberg surpassed the finest European marques—Mercedes-Benz, Isotta-Fraschini, Rolls-Royce, and Hispano-Suiza—in performance and style. Here was a car sporting a 265-horsepower, straight-eight 32-valve engine that reached a top speed of 116 mph (185.6kph) and could hit 90 mph (144kph) in second gear—and that was the unblown J Duesenberg. The supercharged SJ once hit 160 mph (256kph) on the Bonneville Salt Flats.

The Duesenberg ultimately resulted in a financial catastrophe for its makers, and fewer than 500 J models were built. But it is unlikely that there will ever be a car in this century that can combine power and luxury as effectively as the Duesenberg.

Frederick Samuel Duesenberg was born in Lippe, Germany, in 1876 and emigrated to Iowa as a young man. He received his engineering education through a correspondence school and put his keen mechanical talent to work. By 1906, he had designed the 24-horsepower flat-twin Mason—named after the financial backer of the project—with his brother August. They later developed the Maytag (the name survives today with the washing machine

OPPOSITE: The debut of the 1929 Duesenberg Model J was a stunning departure from the earlier Model A, due in large part to the partnership of E.L. Cord and Frederick Duesenberg. Leading coach builders Derham, Holbrook, and Murphy all had a crack at creating bodies for these mobile palaces. ABOVE: The Model J inspired imitators worldwide with its V-shaped radiator, sweeping crest, and delicate curves. Coach builders capitalized on the Model J's mammoth proportions, huge taillight ensemble, oversized headlights, and front-fender summits.

company). The Mason and Maytag were precursors to the Deusenbergs' efforts at building a racing engine in 1912. Two years later, the brothers moved to Saint Paul, Minnesota. By 1916, they had developed an engine that used four valves for each cylinder instead of two. It would serve as a harbinger for an 8-cylinder, 32-valve version more than a decade later.

As the United States entered World War I, the Duesenbergs moved their operation to Elizabeth, New Jersey, and set up a plant to construct engines for aircraft, boats, and tractors. Their biggest contract came from the government to build a new Bugatti 16-cylinder, 500-horsepower aircraft engine.

After the war, they designed a 183-cubic-inch straight-eight engine. The Duesenberg engines went on to win the Indianapolis 500 three times during the 1920s, and they powered the only American car to win the French Grand Prix in 1921.

The brothers were also eager for their share of the passenger car market. They saw no future in producing 4-cylinder engines, so they sold their Elizabeth plant and moved to Indianapolis—an appropriate site, given their passion for automotive racing.

What emerged from their first crack at a passenger car was the Model A Duesenberg. Debuting at the New York Auto Salon in December 1920, the Model A was an improved version of a racing car. The Duesenbergs were already establishing standards that other automakers were forced to follow. The Model A featured a 260-cubic-inch straight-eight engine that made extensive use of aluminum. It also offered four-wheel hydraulic brakes—the first on any car—on a 134-inch wheelbase. Every aspect of design in the Model A was geared for rapid acceleration and high speed. It was the Model A, not the J model that would appear later under E. L. Cord's direction, that was Fred Duesenberg's true high-performance car. The Model J emphasized luxury, not road racing.

But a technologically advanced passenger car did not mean profits. Even the brothers' reputation as skilled designers of America's foremost racing engines did not help sales. For one thing, a German name did not sit particularly well with the American public in the years following World War I. And, although Europeans had always put great stock in high-performance cars, Americans couldn't care less. Automotive racing in the United States was frequently viewed as a noisy, death-defying novelty. The automobile's price tag did not help, either. The Model A went for $6,500, and only five hundred models were sold through 1926. Further hindered by their lack of business sense, the Duesenberg brothers were doomed to failure.

ABOVE: Regal if not opulent, the 1931 Duesenberg Torpedo Phaeton typifies 1930s nouveau riche excess. The bare chassis for this 1931 specimen sold for $8,500, nearly nine times the average cost of a complete car from any other maker. These grand carriages used the finest fabrics, leathers, and woods for the interior. OPPOSITE: This Walker-LeGrande SJ displays Duesenberg's move toward a lower and more streamlined body, with a rounded rear torpedo deck and enclosed trunk for luggage. The SJ designation is for the super-charger, introduced in 1932, that supposedly attained 320 horsepower and reached speeds of up to 130 mph (208kph). Few, if any, Duesies, could live up to that claim.

They found their salvation in E. L. Cord. The boy wonder of Auburn purchased the Duesenberg Company in 1926.

Duesenberg and Cord needed each other. Duesenberg required the financial backing to keep his prized engineering masterpiece on the road. Cord wanted an automobile that was even more unorthodox than his Auburn.

Flush from his success with rescuing Auburn from imminent demise, Cord wanted to combine majestic power with elegance. Nothing less than the crème de la crème of the automotive world would satisfy him. He wanted to target a specific clientele: the rich.

While Cord wanted a luxury car, Fred Duesenberg wanted a small car that approached the concept of a Bugatti. But Cord would have none of it. The two struck a compromise, resulting in an automobile that combined high performance with luxury.

When Cord took control of the company, he immediately named Fred Duesenberg vice president of Engineering and Experimental Laboratories at Duesenberg, Inc. The new responsibilities allowed Fred to concentrate solely on mastering the engineering principles of his beloved cars.

The Model X was then introduced, with a 135-inch wheelbase and a straight-eight that was boosted from 88 to 100 horsepower. But the X was not what Cord had in mind. He wanted something bigger, grander, and finer than anything on the road.

The Model J, introduced on December 1, 1928, at the New York Auto Salon, was offered in a 142.5- and a 153.5-inch wheelbase. Its exotic coachwork surrounded a massive chassis and the largest power plant produced in the company's history. The chassis, which was rigid for better cornering capabilities, weighed a whopping 4,450 pounds. In addition, the 420-cubic-inch straight-eight engine was huge, measuring 4 feet (1.2m) long. Duesenberg used heat-treated aluminum wherever possible to keep the weight of the car within reason. The firewall, differential housing, differential housing cover, flywheel housing, oil pan, timing chain covers, camshaft covers, pistons, connecting rods, and dashboard, among dozens of other parts, were all made of aluminum, at great expense.

The basic chassis in 1929 and 1930 cost as much as $8,500, and jumped to $9,500 in 1931. Coach builder Walter M. Murphy produced some of the more inexpensive bodies for Duesenberg, which cost between $2,500 and $3,500 for a coupe. Murphy manufactured about 125 bodies, many of them convertible coupes, closed sedans, and speedsters. The average price for the total package probably started around $17,000, with a few going for $20,000. Perhaps a small fraction sold for $25,000, but there is no evidence that any sold for $50,000 as was widely reported for many years.

The coachwork was imposing, whether it was a roadster or double cowl phaeton. In fact, by today's standards, the cars were huge. Many of today's passenger cars barely reach the top of the doors of a Duesenberg convertible. Driving behind a Duesie on the road in a contemporary car can be intimidating—trailing cars can see little of the roadway from behind one of these behemoths.

Six months before the New York show, Duesenberg sought proposed body designs from the country's leading coach builders, based on chassis specifications. Derham, Holbrook, LeBaron, and Murphy performed most of the coachwork for the New York show.

Duesenberg manufactured only chassis, with the coachwork built to order by the buyer or in very small lots. Other coach builders that enjoyed a relationship with Duesenberg were Judkins,

ABOVE: No other car bespoke pure luxury like the Dual Cowl Phaeton SJ. Its precision building can't be ignored. The frame was nearly nine inches deep and about a quarter-inch thick. Duesenberg had to make up for its tremendous weight by using aluminum alloy in numerous parts, including the instrument panel, steering column, pistons, and connecting rods, to name just a few. OPPOSITE TOP: The Model J, such as this 1929 version, was actually conceived in 1926, when E.L. Cord joined Frederick and August Duesenberg. Together, they combined two dreams. The Duesenbergs wanted a lighter car that could be competitive on the race track, while Cord wanted luxury. The result was a truly luxurious car that could generate 265 horsepower and hit 116 mph (185.6kph). OPPOSITE BOTTOM: The 1931 Duesenberg J Torpedo Phaeton was constructed a year before Fred Duesenberg died. The Torpedo Phaeton was perhaps one of the last models built that reflected Fred Duesenberg's vision of supreme performance and elegant styling. In 1932, the year of Fred's death, Duesenberg began to drift away from strict adherence to Fred's vision, as owners requested alterations such as superchargers and updated equipment.

Hibbard & Darrin, Barker, Weymann, Gurney Nutting, Bohmann & Schwartz, Letourneur & Marchand, Graber, D'Ieteren Frères, and the Duesenberg-owned La Grande.

The Derham Body Company of Pennsylvania produced some of the most stunning work for Duesenberg. Some early Derham versions of the Model J did not include radiator shutters, mounted horn trumpets, or the radiator mascot, which typified other coachwork. This understated touch was stunning because it differed from the more lavish—and heavy-handed—designs.

Holbrook of Hudson, New York, had only a brief relationship with the company before going out of business in 1929. But Holbrook produced some fine examples of formal town cars that featured leather roofs, roll-up windows, and permanent side channels fitted to the front doors.

Murphy was perhaps the most popular of the coach builders associated with Duesenberg. He also built models with leather roofs, including a series of sport sedans. Many of the early Model Js were not equipped with extraneous molding and other garish features, sending a message of understated elegance to the public. Later Model Js did not follow that theme.

Whether they were early Model Js or later versions, all were ultra-luxury carriages. Some models were constructed with the most exotic woods and finest leathers and broadcloth available. A wet bar, vanity table, and rear instrument panel could be found in some town cars. It was not far-fetched to have a car upholstered in silk and trimmed in ivory and silver fittings or featuring solid gold hardware and inlaid mosaic wood.

The instrument panel was clearly designed to enhance its high-performance image. Scattered across the dashboard were a 150 mph speedometer, tachometer, barometer, brake-pressure gauge, a combination clock and stopwatch, gasoline gauge, and water temperature gauge.

A rare feature never again seen on American cars was a complex set of warning lights for the driver. A "timing box" was located in the engine compartment, which automatically lubricated the chassis every 75 miles (120km) at its greasing points. A red light glowed when the system was working, and a green light went on when the lubricant reservoir was empty. A third light glowed every 700 miles (1,120km) to tell the operator to change the motor oil. At 1,400-mile (2,240km) intervals, a fourth light reminded the driver to check the battery water level.

If the stock market crash of 1929 had not happened, Duesenberg undoubtedly would have been successful. E. L. Cord

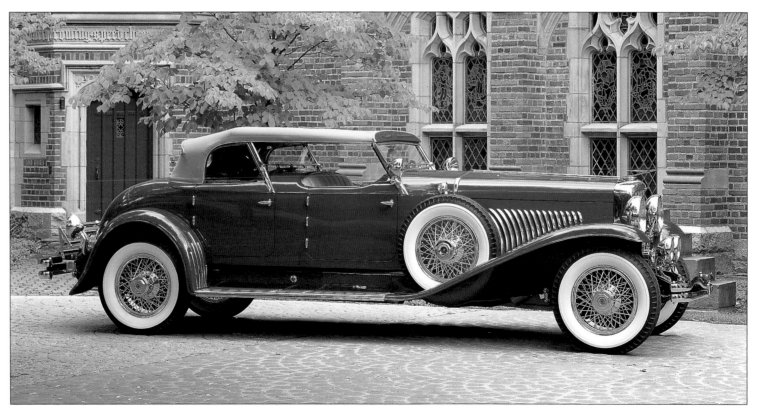

made every effort to attract the wealthy—full-page advertisements in such upscale magazines as *Vanity Fair* featured a pipe-smoking young gentleman in a smoking jacket seated in front of a massive fireplace. The ad read: "He Drives a Duesenberg."

E. L. Cord left no doubt as to who his intended market was. But debates have raged over the decades about Duesenberg's engine performance. Generally, the Model J and the later SJ have been considered the most powerful vehicles of their day. The British automotive press has long dismissed Duesenberg speed records as American fantasy, but even at the most conservative estimates, the Duesenberg still outclassed its European competitor in performance.

Automobile Quarterly reported in 1972 that Fred Duesenberg had asserted that his unsupercharged Model J wielded 265 horsepower at 4,250 rpm—a mighty steep claim, which many Duesenberg detractors sought to disprove. Duesenberg factory documents show that the J had actually achieved 265 horsepower. But power from the engine depended on customer specifications, which were very costly. The Model J's straight-eight more than likely averaged between 245 and 250 horsepower with a compression ratio of 5.2 to 1. Comparable automobiles, like Europe's Hispano-Suiza, Delage, and Isotta-Fraschini, could not compete with Duesenberg's power. Hispano-Suiza offered a 9.4-liter, 12-cylinder engine with a compression ratio of 5 to 1 that provided surprisingly conservative horsepower of 190. With the 6 to 1 compression ratio, its engine was boosted to 220 horsepower, still considerably less than the American competitor, according to *Automobile Quarterly*.

The motoring public believed that they had found the limit in performance with the Model J. They were probably startled in 1932 when Duesenberg introduced its Model SJ (S for "supercharger"), an automobile whose flamboyance displayed arrogance on the part of Cord, who was introducing this extremely ostentatious car in the midst of the Depression.

The SJ featured a vertical centrifugal blower that operated at five times engine speed, producing an output of 320 horsepower with 104 mph (166.4kph) in second gear and a top speed of 140 mph (224kph). A roadster with a 142.5-inch wheelbase could go from 0 to 100 mph (0 to 160kph) in seventeen seconds.

ABOVE: Measuring four feet (1.2m) long from fan to flywheel, the J Lycoming straight-eight engine is a powerplant of mammoth proportions. It was the largest engine ever installed in an American car, displacing 420 cubic inches and using twin overhead camshafts and a then-unheard-of thirty-two valves, four per cylinder. OPPOSITE: The 1932 Model J by Walter M. Murphy was perhaps one of the most popular bodies ever put on a Duesenberg chassis. Long a favorite with customers, Murphy coach builders produced an astounding 125 bodies over a three-year period.

With the addition of the blower (in classic car parlance, a blown automobile is supercharged and an unblown one is not), Fred Duesenberg had to come up with another way to route his exhaust system. He did this by bringing four chromed flexible downpipes out of each side of the hood. These fancy exhaust pipes were common in Europe but new in the United States.

The SJ lived up to its reputation. In late 1934, test racer Ab Jenkins took an SJ with a streamlined body to the Bonneville Salt Flats. He averaged 152 mph (243.2kph) over one hour, then ran over a twenty-four-hour period at 135 mph (216kph). At one point in 1935, the SJ squared off with Zeppo Marx's blown Mercedes-Benz in a 25-mile (40km) race, with the Duesie winning handily. The SJ is considered today the fastest luxury car ever built. About thirty-five SJs were manufactured between May 1932 and late 1936. Some may originally have been J models with blowers fitted later.

The future of the Duesenberg automobiles was doomed when Fred Duesenberg was fatally injured in July 1932, skidding off a road in Pennsylvania in an early SJ phaeton. Although Fred's only

duty during Cord's presidency was engineering, he had been the heart and soul of the company. It was as if the company did not have the energy to go on.

Part of Duesenberg's problems had begun with the SJ, which was popular among loyal Duesenberg owners. People who had the Model Js wanted their cars fitted with the SJ chromed exhaust pipes. While their orders were being filled, they also began asking for their Model Js to be updated in appearance. The result was haphazard at best. Subsequent styling motifs had no theme. With no systematic modernization of the original models, many Duesenbergs—and there were not that many to begin with—lost their unique identities.

Perhaps an outgrowth of the automaker's unpredictable styling was the production of the rarest Duesenberg: the SSJ, the only version that can be described as a sports car. Only two specials were built, with a 125-inch wheelbase by La Grande. Their owners were Gary Cooper and Clark Gable. The SSJ designation was given to the car by historians, not Duesenberg.

Another low-production model was the JN. Debuting in 1935, this model had a 153.5-inch wheelbase and 17-inch instead of 19-inch wheels. Only ten were manufactured, and each sported Rollston coachwork. Two of these JN models were supercharged, giving them the SJN designation. In all, somewhere between 470 and 480 J models were built, including the SJ, JN, and SSJ versions.

Few aficionados would argue with Cord's assertion that he offered "the world's finest motor car." So it was a sad day when Duesenberg closed its doors in 1937 as Cord's empire folded. German artist Rudolf Bauer ordered the last Duesenberg that year. It was assembled at a Chicago Duesenberg dealership after the Indianapolis plant shut down. It was not until 1940 that Bauer claimed his automobile and had a four-door convertible sedan body placed on top of the chassis. It cost Bauer $21,000.

August Duesenberg attempted to revive the marque in 1947, but could not generate enough interest. Efforts in 1966 and 1980 also failed.

And perhaps it is just as well. Duesenberg, with its flashy opulence and excessive power, belonged in the 1920s and 1930s, which witnessed unlimited horizons.

Lincoln

NEVER COMFORTABLE IN HIS FATHER'S SHADOW, EDSEL FORD SAW AN OPPORTUNITY TO PUT HIS OWN STAMP ON A FORD PRODUCT

that would make a lasting impression on the luxury automobile market.

Henry Ford probably could not have cared less. He often belittled his son's work in a misguided attempt to make him a stronger

businessman and automaker. But it seemed that Edsel could never quite measure up. So it was with great satisfaction that Edsel

found his niche as president of the Lincoln division of the Ford Motor Company. He could focus his energies on design, while his

father continued his preoccupation with engineering.

Edsel Ford's most significant creation was essentially what was to become the last classic of the era—the Lincoln Continental.

The Continental enjoyed a nine-year run and is remembered as Lincoln's most enduring model. But Edsel left his mark on virtually

all Lincolns produced after Ford's purchase of the company from Henry and Wilford Leland in 1922. Ford transformed a precision-

made, but rather nondescript, luxury car into a strong competitor that rivaled Cadillac, Packard, and Pierce-Arrow.

When Lincoln was purchased by the Fords, it had a solid foundation in automotive engineering. The company was founded by

Henry Leland after he left Cadillac in 1917. Leland named his new company Lincoln in recognition of the president he had cast his

OPPOSITE: The 1933 Lincoln KA Dual Cowl Phaeton sold new for $3,200, and only a dozen or so were produced. The year 1933 marked the first year that Lincoln introduced a small V12 with a 382-cubic-inch displacement instead of the 447 cubic inches displaced by the K models of the previous year. The same year also signaled the end of Lincoln's traditional styling, as Edsel Ford began to focus on a more streamlined body.

ABOVE: Introduced in September 1920 for the 1921 model year, the Lincoln Coupe was dowdy and uninspired in design, hardly the luxury car to attract a new generation of young drivers. Founder Henry Martyns Leland gave up his dream car in 1922 when he sold his company to Ford. RIGHT: The styling of the 1926 Lincoln Model L contrasts sharply from the earlier Leland models. Stylist Raymond Dietrich, lured to Detroit by Edsel Ford, was largely responsible for the lower and more stylish offerings.

first vote for in 1864. He won a contract to build 6,000 Liberty aviation engines for the war effort and a $10 million advance. But the war was soon over, and Leland was facing a 6,000 man workforce and mounting debts. He immediately put up $6.5 million worth of stock for sale and sold it within three hours. But the obstacles to making Lincoln a success turned out to be insurmountable.

Mechanically, the Lincoln Model L introduced in 1920 was a superior vehicle. Leland developed a precision-built V8 engine similar to what he had produced with Cadillac. This compact 358-cubic-inch engine with fork-and-blade connecting rods developed 81 braking horsepower and could easily manage 70 mph. But coach design was an entirely different matter. Leland had always believed that engineering would sell the car to the public. Convinced that automotive luxury was tied to reliability and performance, he woefully underestimated the selling power of looks.

Styling of the Model L was strictly prewar. Although much of the post–World War I styling of American cars was uninspiring, the Lincoln was reminiscent of the old-fashioned carriages. It was not greeted well at the dawn of the flapper era.

Leland sank further into fiscal trouble when production for the 1920 model was postponed from January until September because of late deliveries of parts and the automaker's preoccupation with perfection. Leland missed the selling season, but was ready just in time for the postwar recession. He had hoped to sell 6,000 cars in 1920, but business sagged, and he managed to sell only 3,407 by February 4, 1922.

Meanwhile, Henry Ford was looking for an automobile that was significantly different from his Model T. Edsel Ford was probably more intrigued with the possibilities, given his refined sense of style and aesthetics, He quickly realized as he began to learn the

automotive trade that a car could be a thing of beauty as well as an engineering marvel. There was no reason to deny a mechanically perfect automobile a visually appealing body. He understood, far better than his father did, that from a marketing standpoint, developing an attractive luxury car was every bit as important as perfecting the V8 engine.

Edsel's artistic eye and his father's stubborn conviction that his beloved Model T could go on forever without a single change in body style led to a divisive relationship. But Edsel, a gentleman who respected Henry's engineering feats, continued to work in his father's shadow.

However, Edsel did convince his father that the Lincoln company was a bargain—something Henry Ford could not pass up. The Fords paid $4 million for Lincoln, much to the Lelands' disappointment. The Lelands believed that their company was worth as much as ten times the selling price. The rift between the Fords and Lelands widened further when the latter won a court settlement for an additional $4 million. Although the Lelands hoped to stay on at Lincoln as managers of the division, they were replaced.

The Fords immediately abandoned the archaic body designs and replaced them with attractive styles. Prices were slashed to move the units quickly, and $2 million worth of orders were taken. Ford sold 5,512 Lincolns just ten months after the acquisition. (All Lincolns manufactured between the time Henry Leland founded the company and 1927 were identified in automotive circles as "Leland Lincolns" to make the distinction from the later "Ford Lincolns."

Under Ford, the Lincoln continued to improve. Aluminum pistons were used, and the wheelbase was increased from 130 to 136 inches. The car immediately attracted the attention of police departments and gangsters alike. The Detroit Police Flying Squad thought so highly of the car that they made it a regular feature in their fleet in 1924. Ford provided those cars with four-wheel brakes, which weren't standard until 1927. Some Lincoln police cars were equipped with twin spotlights, shotgun racks, and bullet-proof glass.

But the key to Lincoln's success lay in its body styling. Edsel changed production processes for the Lincoln and limited the con-

veyor-belt assembly-line procedure made famous by his father. With limited production, Edsel could focus on quality styling and precision work. Lincoln's standard bodies were styled by Brunn. Custom coach building was performed by LeBaron, Judkins, Fleetwood, Dietrich, Willoughby, and Locke.

Edsel personally approved all custom body designs and demanded that Lincoln's high body construction standards were enforced. These standards were far above those of the coach builders, who nonetheless conformed to produce Edsel's vision. Coach builders were required to use the finest hardwood, cast all hardware in bronze, and manufacture all body panels in aluminum.

Edsel also developed the custom body catalog system, which allowed customers to choose basic custom body styles, then specify the details and finish for the car. These basic body styles were usually manufactured in lots of ten or twenty-five units.

The new Lincoln—still on a Model L chassis—became the darling of academics, doctors, and lawyers who demanded to drive the best vehicle on the road, but did not want to flaunt their high station in society. More than 17,000 Model L cars were sold in 1925 and 1926, a stunning turnaround for a marque that was on the verge of insolvency.

Yet Edsel still saw room for improvement. Although custom coach builders were successful in producing prettier Lincolns, Edsel recognized that artistry was their primary concern, and that something more was needed. So in 1925, he recruited Raymond H. Dietrich, cofounder of the "automotive architecture" concept. Dietrich believed that body design should be integrated with performance. Edsel lured him away from LeBaron to establish his own coach-building company, which would become Dietrich Inc. The stylist soon began developing lower and lighter bodies for the Model L chassis.

Because of Dietrich and other coach-builders, design themes became the rage during the mid-1920s. Color schemes were inspired by exotic birds. Exterior and interior schemes were inspired by Renaissance, Gothic, and Egyptian motifs.

The Model L was beautiful, but its styling lacked the clean, flowing lines of its competitors. And in terms of speed, it was much slower than Cadillac, Chrysler, or Packard. Henry Leland's V8 served Lincoln well between 1920 and 1932, but it was time for a change. Although Lincoln phased out the Model L in 1930, the engine would be manufactured for another two years.

The Model K was introduced in 1931. This new vehicle was served by the Leland V8 with some slight changes. A higher com-

The 1932 Lincoln KB V12 garnered considerable attention with its massive 448-cubic-inch engine that provided 150 horsepower and topped speeds of 90 mph (144kph). These models, such as this Coupe, were rugged and powerful, and displayed Edsel Ford's desire for understated elegance.

pression ratio and a downdraft carburetion and manifolding system boosted the horsepower to an impressive 120. The most dramatic change in the Lincoln, however, was the Model K's innovative double drop frame, which provided a lower body and stretched the wheelbase to 145 inches.

The new wheelbase was a boon to custom coach builders who lamented the previous 136-inch wheelbase as too small for their elaborate design schemes. The result was the sale of 3,311 units in 1931 with 265 custom-built coaches. These numbers, down only slightly from the 3,515 units sold in 1930, were not bad, considering that the United States was in the midst of the Depression.

But the K was quickly forgotten in 1932 with the introduction of the 12-cylinder KB. This model finally joined the ranks of other V12 models by Auburn, Cadillac, Franklin, Packard, and Pierce-Arrow. The 448-cubic-inch V12 provided 150 braking horsepower at 3,400 rpm.

The KB featured work by a variety of coach builders. Some of the most popular models were the custom-built Walter M. Murphy sports roadster, the Brunn cabriolet and brougham, the Willoughby panel brougham and limousine, and the Dietrich coupe and convertible sedan.

Lincoln offered V8s in the 1933 KA models, which, in response to the Depression, was priced lower than the KB models. The KA sold for a base price of $2,900 and was offered in seven standard body styles. Set on a 136-inch wheelbase chassis, the KA had a sharply pointed grille, single-piece front and rear bumpers, and hood shutters that were thermostatically controlled. The V8 boosted its power, this time to 125 horsepower.

That model, however, proved to be the end of the era for the classic V8 with fork-and-blade connecting rods. The 1933 KA and KB models now both featured V12 engines. The KA model featured a 382-cubic-inch engine with a rated horsepower of 125 at 3,400 rpm, while the KB engine offered a 447-cubic-inch engine with 150 braking horsepower at 3,400 rpm.

The 1933 models also came with a new look. Gone were the Murphy Roadster and the splendid Waterhouse Convertible Victoria, because most coach builders went out of business. But Lincoln adapted some styling designs from Cadillac and took them a step further, featuring dipped windowsill lines on the sedans and fenders that were lengthened, swept backward, and skirted.

Despite these offerings, only 1,420 KAs and 587 KBs were sold in 1933. The sales did not justify the expense of producing two different engines in a luxury car market during the darkest

OPPOSITE: This 1935 Lincoln V12 Phaeton illustrates Edsel Ford's move to more streamlined bodies. Most noticeable are the bullet-shaped headlights, diagonally cut fenders, and the radiator lacquered the same color as the body. The 136- and 145-inch wheelbase moved the engine forward, shortened the hood, and provided better weight distribution. ABOVE: In 1934 Lincoln returned to the K series designation for the first time since 1931, with cars such as this 1934 four-door Phaeton V12. It looked nothing like the old K series, but was actually a consolidation of the KA and KB models. As luxury car sales plummeted, Lincoln decided not only to merge the KA and KB, but also to offer only one V12, a 414-cubic-inch, 150-horsepower unit with aluminum cylinder heads.

days of the Depression. By 1934, Lincoln merged the KA and KB and dropped both engines in favor of a 414-cubic-inch, 150-horsepower V12 power plant with aluminum cylinder heads. Lincoln kept the separate wheelbases.

The year 1934 marked the first time Lincoln lacquered its radiators in body color. The sedans and limousines departed significantly from previous body styles by featuring long sloping tails, but Lincoln refused at that time to change the sweeping "ogee curve" fenders that typified the classic era. Nevertheless, teardrop fenders debuted two years later with a new radiator grille, larger hubcaps, and new disc wheels.

Edsel Ford, however, began to lose interest in the K models and put little capital into improving them. Looking for other chal-

lenges, he briefly became interested in a special rear-engine design being experimented with by the Briggs Manufacturing Company. But Ford production engineers determined that it was impossible to fit the car into either the Ford or Lincoln price ranges. Ford could have created a new series, as it did later with the Mercury, but the idea was rejected. Briggs then modified the design extensively and moved the engine to the front. Born from the ashes of Briggs' radical suggestion was the Lincoln Zephyr.

The Zephyr was designed by John Tjaarda, using aircraft construction principles. It was introduced in 1936 and was priced to compete with the medium-priced Packard 120, LaSalle, and Chrysler Airflow. Although the Zephyr is not considered a classic car, it is perhaps one of the first examples of streamlining. It also

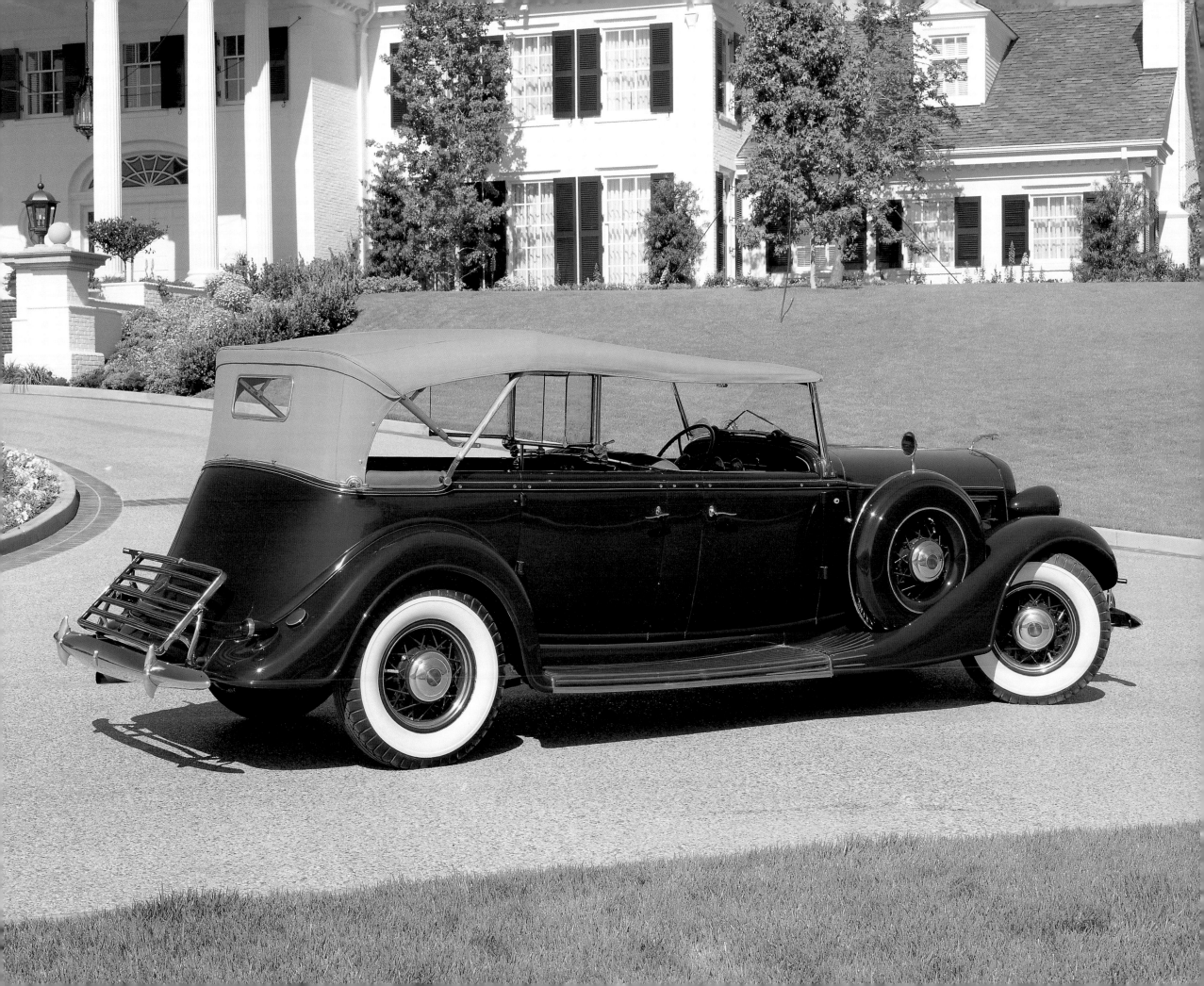

confirmed that Edsel Ford was a visionary in automotive design. He also knew what the public wanted.

Ford engineers had initially hoped to power the 3,300-pound (1,485kg) car with a modified V8, but Edsel vetoed the idea, believing that only a V12 could do the job. Given time and cost constraints, Ford developed a rather uninspiring 267-cubic-inch, 110 horsepower engine. It was an L-head V12 with four main bearings that earned the nickname "12-cylinder Ford V8." The Zephyr was built by the Briggs Company with Ford installing only the drivetrain, hood, fenders, and trim.

Edsel's next project was the Continental. Both the Continental and the Zephyr were perfect examples of Edsel's authority over design at his father's company. He was free to work on his own project with little interference from his father or the plant's production executives. He left the actual design to his stylist, E. T. "Bob" Gregorie, and his staff, but acted as styling editor, using his artistic talent and good taste to create a vision that was carried out by his staff. The result was stunning work—the Continental. Edsel had recently returned from Europe and had been impressed with the European sports cars. He wanted a car of European design, or what he called the "continental" look.

The Continental was an outgrowth of the Zephyr and actually began as a personal toy for Edsel. It was a single hand-built car produced simply to please himself.

In November 1938, Gregorie finished designing the Continental, which featured a body with long, low styling, the result of a 4-inch strip cut out of the doors and body. It looked lower, but the ground clearance was similar to that of the Zephyr. Edsel's custom car was completed the following March and shipped down to his Florida retreat, where it caused an immediate and tremendous sensation.

Edsel initially decided to market the automobile as a Zephyr. In October 1939, the Continental cabriolet—made primarily of Zephyr components—was introduced to the public at the Ford Rotunda in Dearborn. It was featured as a Lincoln Continental Zephyr. A coupe debuted in May 1940, but the Zephyr name was dropped by September.

Ford sold 1,990 Continentals before World War II broke out and put a halt to automobile manufacturing. Production resumed in 1946 and ended in 1948. In all, 5,322 Continentals were manufactured. But Edsel Ford died in May 1943, and the heart and spirit of the Continental, an automobile that bespoke beauty and understated class, died with him.

Born from the low-priced Lincoln Zephyr, the 1940 Lincoln Continental replaced the Big K series models. Identified first as the Continental Cabriolet Zephyr, the "Zephyr" was dropped in September 1940 and the car became known simply as the Lincoln Continental. The model carried many of the characteristics of European cars that Edsel Ford found so appealing. The Continental became a trademark of luxury that continues today.

EDSEL FORD

There were few corporate chiefs in the automotive industry during the classic car era who could with any truth call themselves stylists.

Engineering, design and performance—these were the qualities that mattered most to the likes of Henry Leland, E.L. Cord, Frederick Royce, and Ettore Bugatti.

While many automakers considered their cars things of beauty as well as technical achievements, the task of coming up with beautiful designs was usually left to custom coach builders. During the early years, this resulted in styling that put an emphasis on the passenger portion of an automobile with little thought to merging it with the part of the car from the cowl forward. Designing cars as a whole was not considered.

Edsel Ford, president of the Ford Motor Company since 1919, stood virtually alone among American automakers in recognizing that his cars should also be regarded as an object of art as well as a vehicle performance and reliability.

With the reluctant backing of his father, Henry Ford, Edsel help revolutionize the automotive industry by transforming Henry Leland's dowdy Lincolns into refined beauty. Lincoln's Apple Annie had suddenly become the Gloria Swanson of automobiles. He firmly believed that Detroit automakers needed to be closer to their coachbuilders since most were located in New York and Philadelphia. He lured Raymond H. Dietrich, the cofounder of automotive architecture, with a huge Lincoln design contract. He pioneered the use of custom coach catalogs for Lincoln customers and demanded the highest standards in building bodies.

It was a rare thing to have a Detroit automaker take such bold steps to ensure that his automobiles were the best that money can buy in style, comfort and luxury.

Many historians over the years have heaped tremendous credit on LeBaron Inc., Brewster & Co., and the Derham Body Co., among others for body style innovations. But Edsel Ford deserves the lion's share of the credit for recognizing that performance and styling need not be mutually exclusive.

It's unfortunate that Edsel Ford grew up the son of one of America's foremost inventors. Henry Ford was a man not given to sharing accolades with anybody.

Edsel Ford was born on November 6, 1893, in his parents' two-story brick house in what would become the heart of Detroit's business district. Henry Ford was working as an obscure $30-a-week mechanic for the Detroit-Edison Co. and tinkering with his horseless carriage in his spare time.

Gentle, sensitive, and artistic, Edsel literally grew up in the automotive business, knowing from a very early age that he was destined to follow his father's footsteps. He attended Detroit public schools and later the Detroit university school before dropping out to join his father. He wanted to go into business right away "because further schooling would be a waste of time." It's likely that father simply wanted Edsel to begin with him immediately.

It appeared that Edsel, who adored his father, was willing to take much punishment from him in the form of public ridicule and

Edsel Bryant Ford, right, and his father, Henry, had a tenuous relationship after Edsel assumed the presidency of the Ford Motor Co. in 1919. Edsel was responsible for changing the Lincoln from an unattractive car to one of the best examples of automotive art. He also persuaded his father to abandon the Model T and put an end to the disastrous automobile workers' strike in the late 1930s. He died in 1943, shortly after this photograph was taken.

humiliation in front of employees. But this abuse undoubtedly took its toll. In photographs of him, particularly during the years shortly before his death in 1943, one gets the impression he had been kicked in the stomach one too many times. Nevertheless, he took on his role in his father's company with unbridled enthusiasm.

In 1912, he went to work at the Highland Park plant as a workman. He was later promoted to designer, then secretary.

In a move that stunned the industry, Henry Ford resigned as president of the Ford Motor Co., named Edsel its president and turned over his stock—58.5 percent—to him.

John and Horace Dodge, founders of the Dodge automotive empire and Ford shareholders, sued Henry Ford for withholding dividends that Ford wished to put back into the company.

The lawsuit, which infuriated Ford, was the catalyst for the move that put Edsel in the top spot. Naturally, it was in title only. It was still dad's company.

There were two issues that concerned Edsel Ford during the twenties. One was reviving the mundane Lincoln and the other was convincing his father to abandon the archaic Model T. The former proved considerably easier than the latter.

Both of these issues would lead to a wide gulf between the father and son that was repaired with varying success over the years but never to the complete satisfaction of both men.

Edsel Ford's opportunity to shine came in 1922 when he convinced his father to purchase the Lincoln company from its creator, Henry Leland.

In 1922, the Lincoln was a superb mechanical specimen thanks largely to Leland's demand for precision building. But Leland also believed that performance and workmanship should sell the car, not pretty accessories.

Within a year, Edsel dropped the standard 130-inch wheelbase of the Lincoln and replaced it with a wheelbase of 136 inches. Coachbuilders responded with supreme delight. It gave them an additional six inches to experiment with. Edsel looked to Brunn, Fleetwood and Judkins to design the bodies, but he insisted on approving every body style before production. He also demanded the highest quality hardware to complement Leland's perfect jewel of a chassis.

He also provided his customers with a custom body catalog to allow them to choose dozens of different body styles while on the showroom floor. These individual cars were often built in lots of ten or twenty-five, sometimes more depending on their popularity. And since Lincoln was a separate division of Ford that did not

produce cheaper models, he abandoned the assembly-line mentality to have workmen construct one car at a time.

Edsel's insistent demands and high standards in coachbuilding paid off. By 1925, Lincolns sold at a rate of 8,000 a year at a base price of $4,500. It soon became the darling of the lower echelon of the wealthy.

Even with sales skyrocketing, Edsel saw the need to bring coachbuilders closer to the original product. His move to bring Dietrich to Detroit created a stir in the industry. Other automakers followed suit by bringing their own stylists in-house.

Meanwhile, Edsel was alarmed with the number of Ford defections to Chevrolet and other marques. Lincolns didn't go to the Ford dealers because these sellers were ill-equipped to handle the large luxury cars. But to have dealers flee was cause for concern. The Model T, created and maintained by Henry Ford since 1908, was now considered obsolete, both in styling and engineering. Henry Ford preferred to keep his beloved Model T and manage a minor facelift every year but the motoring public looked across the other side of the fence and liked what they saw in Chevrolet, Studebaker and other low-priced cars.

Edsel had become so vocal about the need to change to a new model that his father burst a bubble, ordering him to a remote Ford post in California. Henry settled down and Edsel never left, but the rift between father and son was widening. Henry, however, was beginning to succumb to his son's logic.

Plans were laid in early 1927 for the Model A. The Model A engine was somewhat similar to that of the Model T, but with many improvements. It was an L-head, 4-cylinder job with a water pump to replace the antiquated thermosyphon and battery distribution ignition to replace the magneto and vibrator coil that had started the Model T's engine. Its displacement was enlarged to 200.5 cubic inches compared to the T's 176.7. A zenith carburetor replaced the Holley. The wheelbase was 103 inches.

The verbal sparring between father and son over the changeover was history, and Henry Ford embraced his son's new creation. The Model A wasn't radically different from the T but yielded a softer, more stylish design that made the T look like a worn-out spinster in comparison. The Model A's beauty lay in its elegant simplicity.

The two men, however, suffered through another hellish rift when the Ford plant was beset with a crippling strike in 1937. While many automakers, most notably General Motors and Chrysler, capitulated to the United Auto Workers, Henry Ford

OPPOSITE: Though the Model A was not radically different from his father's Model T, Edsel Ford demanded that the vehicle, as exemplified by this 1930 Roadster, have free-flowing lines to make an obvious distinction from its predecessor. ABOVE: Perhaps one of the most ubiquitous cars on the road in Depression-era America, the 1930 Model A Ford personified the "every man, every family car." Retaining the essence of the Model T, the Ford was simple in design yet stylish enough to attract thousands of buyers.

would have none of it. When Edsel begged his father to negotiate a contract, he was sharply rebuffed. Finally, in 1941, Edsel convinced Henry to sign the contract. Henry agreed but balked at the last moment, relenting only when his wife, Clara, threatened to leave him.

This typified the relationship between Edsel and Henry. Some give and take, but mostly take from Henry.

By 1943, Edsel was a shell of the man who once seized the opportunity to make the Lincoln his own vision without interference from his father. He had long suffered from stomach ulcers. He eventually contracted cancer and undulant fever and died on May 26, 1943, at the age of forty-nine. His closest friends said his death was really the result of a broken heart.

The New York Times reported, "the nation has suffered a serious loss."

In her book, The Cars That Henry Ford Built, Beverly Rae Kimes best summarized Henry and Edsel's relationship when she wrote, " ... as the advancing years had hardened the father, the son had become the conscience of the company, and a champion of the ideals and progressivism of Henry's own youth."

Packard

O VER THE YEARS, AUTOMOTIVE ENTHUSIASTS HAVE ARGUED VIGOROUSLY AS TO WHETHER PACKARD WAS ONE OF THE LEADING

luxury cars of the classic era.

True, Packard compromised its luxury-car standing in 1935 when, to stay alive during the Depression, it introduced the moderately priced 120. And it did not help that Packard became closely associated with Studebaker during the postwar years.

After its founding in 1899, Packard came out with many firsts. It developed the H-gear slot, which would become a standard on virtually every American car to date. And it manufactured the first mass-produced car to feature a 12-cylinder engine. Styling was always conservative, making the Packard more attractive to the conservative buyer, while the radical designs of other marques satisfied the tastes of the rest of the motoring public.

At the beginning of the classic car era, Packard had a tendency to rest on its laurels, becoming more conservative and less inclined to strive for design achievements. Yet the public's

OPPOSITE: The Eighth Series Packard, such as this 1931 Boattail Speedster, saw the horsepower of the Standard Eight engine boosted to 100. Tires were smaller, and although disc wheels were standard, wire or wood wheels were available as options. Other options included dual sidemount, sidemount covers, bumper guards, and spotlight. ABOVE: The winged mascot of the Eighth Series, Deluxe Eight, and Individual Custom Eight Packards instantly identified the car as a breed apart from its competitors. Raymond Dietrich provided two designs for the Individual Custom Eight, as a Convertible Victoria or a Convertible Sedan, in addition to seven "Custom Made by Packard" styles.

attraction to the Packard could not be denied. Packard represented at least two generations of old money. The Duesenberg smacked of excessive gaudiness to longtime Packard owners, and the Cadillac reeked of nouveau riche. Owner loyalty to Packard was evident through every model year up until the Depression. While other marques were very happy to sell 10,000 units during a calendar year, Packard was selling upward of 30,000 cars. Sales reached more than 52,000 in 1928 and 55,000 in 1930.

Packard began on November 6, 1899, when James Ward Packard and his brother, William Doud Packard, along with George Weiss and William A. Hatcher, constructed their first automobile in the Packard shop in Warren, Ohio, under the name of the Ohio Automobile Company. This car was appropriately dubbed the Model A, and the Packards went on to produce four others that year, followed by forty-nine Model Bs in 1900, a surprisingly high number of units during the automobile industry's infancy.

After less than a year as an automaker, Packard developed the automatic spark advance and the famous H-gear slot. By October 1902, the business had become the Packard Motor Car Company, with the Packard brothers, Weiss, Hatcher, and James P. Gilbert as stockholders. With the formation of the new company, 2,500 additional shares of stock were sold to Henry Joy and his business partners, all of whom were based in Detroit. The company soon moved from Warren to Detroit.

Joy was a wealthy railroad man who reveled in aggressive business practices. For the Packard brothers, their cars were more of a hobby than a business venture. Joy was the real boss of the company and refused to watch other automakers lead the industry.

Joy was annoyed to discover that a car developed by Alexander Winton established a record by driving from San Francisco to New York in sixty-four days. He was determined to establish a reputation of epic proportions. Joy had driver Tom Fetch race a single-cylinder Model F, dubbed the "Old Pacific," in the summer of 1903 from San Francisco to New York in sixty-one days, breaking the Winton record. Another driver, Charles Schmidt, broke a different record a year later by hitting 77.5 mph (124kph) on the straightaways at Daytona.

Packard went on to introduce the Model 30 in 1907 and the Model 18 in 1909. In all, 11,818 of these models were produced through their run. But by this time, the founders of the company were out of the picture as they were becoming more involved in other business ventures. Henry Joy was running the business without the Packard brothers.

OPPOSITE: Introduced in August 1933, this Packard Eight Roadster was one of 5,120 Eleventh Series Eights produced for 1934. There was little difference from the 1933 models, although the new car sported slotted bumpers to simulate the double-bar look. A new heavy-duty generator was added to accommodate a radio, and an angle vent wing was added as well. ABOVE: William D. Packard navigates an early Packard by tiller circa 1900 in front of the Warren, Ohio, plant. The first Packard was completed on November 6, 1899, after William's brother, James, had several problems with a Winton, and thought that he and his brother could build a better car. The result was a car that featured an automatic spark advance and the "H" gear slot that would revolutionized automotive technology.

With a shrewd eye for character, Joy lured Alvan Macauley away from his post as general manager of the Burroughs Adding Machine Company in 1910. Macauley, who was once a patent lawyer, assumed the title of general manager. He began building his own management team by hiring former Burroughs colleague Jesse G. Vincent to supervise Packard's engineering department.

Macauley's conservatism and projection of stability were a sharp contrast to Joy's brashness and willy-nilly management style. The pair were like oil and water, but Joy remained in command of Packard, and the ideas that went into production were his.

Under the leadership of Joy and Macauley, Packard shocked the automotive community by introducing in 1915 the first 12-cylinder engine—the Twin Six—to be installed in mass-produced cars. The new engine was an instant success for Packard, with profits doubling. The company sold 18,572 Twin Six cars in 1916 and

more than 35,000 by the time the engine was discontinued in 1923.

These continuing successes marked Packard's first years in the business and made the company an engineering leader. Packard had always courted the automotive press; no achievement had gone unnoticed by the public. But in 1917, Joy had difficulty convincing the board of directors that the time was ripe for a merger. He lost his bid for expansion and left the company.

With Joy gone, Macauley began to implement his own vision. His goal was to move Packard to the lower-priced niche of the luxury car market. He reduced manufacturing handwork to save money, developed an aggressive advertising campaign, and paid close attention to Packard's dealerships. He wanted all dealerships to be located in the most prestigious locations in major cities and to provide a level of service rivaled only by the factory.

Macauley's becoming company president led to further success for Packard. It introduced the L-head Single Six engine to complement the Twin Six. The Twin Six was replaced in 1924 with the L-head Single Eight. The straight-eight-type engine had been pioneered by Duesenberg in much smaller numbers, but under the efforts of Packard it would become the powerplant mainstay of many American automobiles for years to come. The engine was mounted on a conventional chassis with four-wheel brakes. The new features proved a boon for Packard as sales soared to 32,027 in 1925, twice the production total for 1924.

In August 1926, Packard introduced the Third Series Packard Eight, with its largest straight-eight engine to date. It had a 385-cubic-inch displacement and beat other marques to the showroom. (Late bloomers Pierce-Arrow and Chrysler Imperial offered their straight-eight engines in 1929 and 1931, respectively.) It included several engineering innovations and appeared to be a perfect match for the conservative styling that would later become the Packard trademark.

Packard officials argued that by avoiding radical styling, the car followed a consistent theme one year to the next. It was common for luxury car customers to change body style but retain the same chassis. Packards did not depreciate as their competitors did because Packard's body stylist, Werner Gubitz, avoided radical styling. And Packard design could not be confused with other marques; with its Gothic-shaped radiator and hood, and with the headlights and parking-light rims duplicated in the same style as the grille, the Packard was highly distinctive. Custom body builders had their crack at the Packard, but styling from the cowl forward did not change much over the years.

Yet design was not stodgy. Designer Ray Dietrich added rear quarter windows to his Convertible Victoria styles for Packard as he had with Lincoln and Pierce-Arrow, a new concept in the late 1920s. The best example would be the 1929 Packard DeLuxe Eight Model 645 Dietrich Convertible Victoria. It allowed greater visibility for rear passengers, although at the expense of their privacy.

Coach builder Waterhouse of Webster, Massachusetts, also performed fine work on the Model 845 DeLuxe Eight, with a tall belt line and top that measured 5 feet 6 inches tall. Some cars, at the request of their owners, also featured lighter fender and molding colors.

These styling advances helped Packard toward the end of the decade. The year 1928 marked Packard's biggest selling year before the Depression. The factory was earning as much as $350 per car, while dealerships were taking in about $800 per car. The company reached its peak in sales with $25 million earnings in 1928. The automaker would break its own sales records during the 1930s, but 1928 would be its best year selling only luxury cars.

The year 1928 also saw Packard do away altogether with its 6-cylinder models and inaugurate its Sixth Series line. (Packard ignored model years and instead launched series—the Seventh Series debuted approximately a year later, and the Eighth Series was introduced in 1931. Automobile historians later affixed years to these series to make identification easier.)

When the stock market crashed in 1929, Packard was in deep trouble. Having coasted on its reputation for some time, it had been surpassed by General Motors in performance. Customers were prepared to purchase prettier Cadillac V16s in 1930. Packard customers were not about to be left behind.

The Standard Eight cars provided typical conservative Packard style on shorter wheelbases. Prices ranged from $2,375 to $2,775 for sedans, roadsters, touring cars, phaetons, coupes, convertibles, and limousines. The Speedster Eight was as close to a sports car as Packard would get. It was powered by a 385-cubic-inch, 145-braking horsepower engine on a 134-inch wheelbase. Only 150 were manufactured, and they cost a whopping $5,200 to $6,000. The Speedster was a flop when it came out in 1930, and it disappeared the next year.

As sales plummeted, Packard was desperate to stay afloat. The Twin Six (it was later changed to the Twelve until the end of its production run in 1939) was reintroduced in 1932 to compete with Cadillac. Unlike the original Twin Six, the engine was a solid, durable powerplant designed to operate without noise or vibration

ABOVE: Packard joined the multicylinder club relatively late compared to other luxury automakers, but its V12 was one of the best engineered engines in an American car. Unfortunately, it did little for Packard sales. Like many early 1930s Packards, the V12 Coupe body was adapted from the bodies originally manufactured for Eights. OPPOSITE TOP: This 1934 Packard 12 Dietrich Victoria carried on Raymond Dietrich's theme of incorporating the design element of the forward cowl with the rear portion of the vehicle. This model sits on a 147-inch wheelbase. Seven-passenger and limousine versions were also offered on the same wheelbase. Coach builder LeBaron also offered custom designs for the 1108 models. OPPOSITE BOTTOM: Like the Dietrich victoria, the 1934 V12 Dual Cowl Phaeton sat on a 147-inch wheelbase and was identical mechanically in every way. But the bullet-shaped headlights, modest brightwork, and lacquered radiator provided a more streamlined appearance.

at any speed. A modified L-head, this engine had the valves in the block, but positioned at a 45-degree angle to the axis of the cylinder. These valves would never wear out with standard maintenance. The engine's displacement was 445 cubic inches, producing 160 horsepower at 3,200 rpm. It was boosted to 475 cubic inches in 1935 with 175 horsepower.

The reintroduction of the 12-cylinder engine was part of a plan to develop a front-wheel-drive car. Cornelius Van Ranst, who was part of the team that developed the front-wheel-drive Cord L-29, designed the Packard version. The prototype did quite well on the proving grounds, although more time was needed to work out a number of minor problems. But Macauley did not want to delay production, so the car debuted with the standard rear drive. The Twelve was placed on a chassis with either a 142.5-inch or 147.5-inch wheelbase.

The new 12-cylinder car cost between $3,650 and $7,950 and helped sales only a bit. The automaker's attempt to counter the Depression with the Ninth Series Light Eight also did not do much for sales. Featuring an L-head 319-cubic-inch Straight Eight with 110 horsepower on a 127.6-inch wheelbase, the car was memorable for its sweeping lines and distinctive "shovel nose." It also featured a low windshield and retractable side-window framings, which would be adopted by later Packards as well.

But the Light Eight was too expensive to produce and not cheap enough to attract new customers. Sales were pathetic, and the model lasted less than a year. Only 9,010 cars were sold in 1932. Sales continued with 9,893 units in 1933 and a paltry 6,265 in 1934. The company lost $7 million, largely on account of the failure of the Light Eight, but also because it invested heavily in the soon-to-be-popular Packard 120.

If the company was to survive through 1935, Macauley had to abandon Packard's longstanding blue-chip image and begin to mass-produce smaller, medium-priced cars. Looking to streamline production, Macauley turned to George T. Christopher, a production expert who had retired from General Motors. Christopher overhauled the assembly plant and outfitted it for mass production. Macauley also hired Max Gilman to create a campaign for the new and presumably improved medium-priced car.

On January 6, 1935, the Twelfth Series Packard 120 debuted with rave reviews from the automotive press, and an eager public lined up to buy them. Named for its 120-inch wheelbase, the 120 was available to a new clientele, people who had always wanted to own a Packard but could not afford one. The model, which kept all

OPPOSITE: Perhaps the most stunning model in the Packard line, this 1934 V12 Speedster was designed by coach builder LeBaron. Since before World War I, LeBaron had been designing for such early luxury cars as Locomobile and Wills Ste. Claire. LeBaron designed these cars in small lots, and farmed out the actual construction. ABOVE: Woodlite headlamps, a lacquered radiator, and the notable absence of of brightwork give this 1935 Packard Coupe a certain panache not found on gaudier competitors.

the Packard trademarks from the ox-yoke radiator and hood to the red hexagon wheel hub emblems, sold for $980 to $1,095—plus shipping, preparation, and taxes. Seven body styles were offered on the 120-inch wheelbase: business coupe, convertible, sports coupe, touring coupe, sedan, club sedan, and touring sedan. The engine was a typical L-head Straight Eight cast-iron version with a 257-cubic-inch displacement and 110 braking horsepower at 3,850 rpm. It got good gas mileage and could go from 0 to 60 mph (0 to 96kph) in less than 20 seconds with a top speed of 85 mph (136kph). These cars were given the moniker Junior Packard, and the larger ones were called the Senior series. Nearly 25,000 120s were sold, more than three times the number of other Packard products in 1935.

The luxury Packards were still offered in ten styles. The 1935 models offered a new 5-degree slant to the radiator and pontoon fenders in the rear. Chrome side louvers were also introduced, and sidemounts for the spare tires were an option. If sidemounts were not ordered, the spare was concealed in the sloping rear panel.

The company reached ninth place in production in 1935. Production soared to 81,000 units in 1936 and 110,000 units in 1937. A recession in 1938 saw sales dip to about 50,000 cars, but 1939 brightened with 77,000 cars sold.

If not for the introduction of the Junior Packards in 1935 and their continued success until World War II, Packard would have found itself closing its doors, as many other independent automakers did in these different years.

Production of the Senior 180 Packard ended during World War II. The dies for its body and chassis were sold to the Soviet Union. After World War II, Packard resumed production with 6- and 8-cylinder models, but it was never able to regain the luster of the 1920s and 1930s. The company dropped behind in styling and engineering, and eventually it merged with Studebaker to become the Studebaker-Packard Corporation. In 1962, the Packard name was dropped from the new company, thus ending a sixty-three-year history. In all, Packard had a total output of more than 1.6 million automobiles over its sixty-three-year lifespan.

Pierce-Arrow

IN POST–WORLD WAR I AMERICA, PIERCE-ARROW PROJECTED AN AIR OF SNOBBERY THAT WAS UNSURPASSED BY DUESENBERG, Stutz, and Cord, the leaders of high performance and classic styling. The company eschewed model years in favor of series, as did its competitor Packard, believing its cars were so perfect that model years were unnecessary. Pierce-Arrow also stubbornly hung on to the 6-cylinder engine, while all other prestige marques were powered by 8-cylinder engines of advanced designs.

Virtually every major automaker was doing well in the two years before the Great Depression, but Pierce-Arrow was bordering on bankruptcy. By 1928, it had swallowed its pride and had merged with Studebaker, which put it on the fast track to an early grave.

But Pierce-Arrow's beginning as a prestige car manufacturer was unmatched by any other automaker. With its 1901 debut in Buffalo, New York, the Pierce-Arrow was almost immediately tagged as one of the most revered automobiles. The car was a product of a company that was founded in 1855 to manufacture iceboxes, birdcages, and other household items. By 1896, it had begun selling bicycles, and company treasurer Charles Clifton told principal owner George N. Pierce that automobiles were the future.

Pierce and Clifton recruited David Fergusson to design the company's first engine, and production began in late 1901. One year later, 150 single-cylinder cars were produced. Two-cylinder models were manufactured in 1903. In 1907, a 6-cylinder version was

OPPOSITE: Designed by Philip Wright, a former Murphy man, the 1933 Pierce-Arrow Silver Arrow was the most radical design of its time. Placed on a 134-inch wheelbase on a Pierce-Arrow V12 chassis, its fastback body was totally new. Recessed door handles, shrouded rear wheels, and concealed spare tire mounts added to the mystique of Wright's creation. An unfortunate V-shaped skylight was imposed by Studebaker engineers tinkering with Wright's design.

produced, and in 1909 the automobile's name was changed to Pierce-Arrow.

Although for many years the company clung to some outmoded technology, such as a steering-wheel gear lever and right-hand drive, Pierce-Arrow was the first automaker to make extensive use of aluminum, power braking, and hydraulic tappets. In 1913, it also developed fender headlights. These lights were state-of-the-art in design, jutting from the front of the fenders, while all other cars—whether luxury or modestly priced—still had their headlights mounted on a horizontal bar across the radiator.

By 1915, Pierce-Arrow reigned supreme in the luxury car market, having produced 12,000 automobiles. Its 6-cylinder engines were the largest on the market and were always winners in automobile races through the end of World War I. The marque was popular among the older, wealthier clientele for the engine's reliability and quiet performance. Although Cadillac had already released its famed V8 and Packard had been using its Twin Six for many years, Pierce-Arrow management felt confident that the 6-cylinder engine was the best powerplant available and would prevail over other multicylinder versions.

This philosophy was probably Pierce-Arrow's first mistake. The second was allowing David Fergusson to resign in a huff over a proposal to introduce a sleeve-valve engine. The original Pierce-Arrow management had retired, and Fergusson's successor, Barney Ross, lasted only a few months before he resigned as chief engineer. In 1921, Myron E. Forbes, who had joined the company in 1919 as treasurer, assumed the presidency.

Karl M. Wise took over the duties of chief engineer and provided much-needed stability to the engineering department. He helped Pierce-Arrow make a number of technical advances and improvements over the years.

Before Wise came on board, Pierce developed the Dual-valve Six, which was an attempt to rejuvenate what was a hopelessly outdated T-head 6-cylinder engine. The Dual Six used four valves per cylinder instead of two. In 1920, the company used the T-head design with the Dual Valve 38, thus becoming the only automaker in the country to continue manufacturing T-heads. The Dual Valve 38 provided a 414-cubic-inch engine placed on a 138-inch wheelbase. Its sales were initially good, but the model was soon swallowed up by competitors introducing new luxury programs and better-performing engines.

Pierce-Arrow still clung to the 6-cylinder engine in 1923, when it introduced the Series 80. But this time, the automaker

Pierce-Arrow was facing financial calamity as sales began to drop in the mid-1920s. To reverse this trend the company introduced the Series 80 in 1927. The Series 80 offered four-wheel brakes, and was designed as an inexpensive model compared to the rest of the Pierce-Arrow line, with prices starting at $2,895. The Series 80 sold well, but the company still foundered and was absorbed by Studebaker.

switched to the more common L-head design with a 289-cubic-inch engine on a short 130-inch wheelbase. The model also featured four-wheel braking. Nonetheless, the car offered little more than good transportation. Its styling was not innovative and was rejected by younger buyers who preferred the more exciting Packard.

Priced lower than any other Pierce-Arrow offered at the time, the Series 80 was designed to reverse a downward trend in the company's sales. But this attempt at revitalization failed. By 1927, Pierce-Arrow, struggling with its archaic six, was losing money at an alarmingly rapid rate. Although in 1927 the automaker introduced the Series 81 as a replacement for the 80, sales continued to fall precipitously.

Facing bankruptcy, Pierce-Arrow turned reluctantly to Studebaker. Based in South Bend, Indiana, Studebaker was founded as a covered-wagon builder in the mid-ninteenth century. It built

modest cars at moderate prices. Although it did not offer any luxury models, Studebaker was flourishing in the 1920s and looking to expand. It saw in Pierce-Arrow an opportunity to be associated with a prestige marque. So on August 15, 1928, Studebaker purchased $5.7 million worth of Pierce-Arrow stock.

The move, which simply served as a bandage for Pierce-Arrow's fiscal wounds, would hurt the automaker in the long run, hastening its demise. Nevertheless, Studebaker's enthusiasm translated to immediate changes. Studebaker was wise enough to allow Pierce-Arrow to operate primarily as an independent entity, much like Cadillac's relationship to General Motors. Quality wasn't compromised, but the acquisition might have felt like an insult to Pierce-Arrow's loyal customers. It must have been uncomfortable for a socially conscious Pierce-Arrow owner to walk into a Studebaker showroom and see the new line of cars—something akin to walking into a discount mart in order to purchase a gold Rolex watch.

Sadly, this worked against Pierce-Arrow. When the 1929 models debuted, there was a rumor that the new Pierce-Arrow engines were actually reworked Studebaker blocks. There was no truth to this rumor, though, for Pierce-Arrow had been developing a new engine since long before the merger.

Whatever the case, Models 133 and 143—the numbers denoting their respective wheelbases—debuted in 1929, ran through 1930, and met with great success. It proved to be the company's most successful production year, with 9,840 cars sold.

The improved powerplant made the difference. Pierce-Arrow completely abandoned the T-head engine and embraced a new nine-main-bearing L-head straight-eight that displaced 366 cubic inches at 125 horsepower. It was a remarkable improvement over the 289-cubic-inch L-head six. The crankcase and cylinder-block assembly were cast in a single iron-alloy unit that was lighter than aluminum crankcases. Developed by Karl Wise, the new straight-eight was clearly superior to any other 8-cylinder engine on the market. Not only was it smoother and faster, it also had a longer life than other engines.

The new line came in sixteen body styles for both wheelbases and cost $2,875 for the Roadster, $3,325 for the Tonneau Cowl Phaeton, and $8,200 for the French Brougham. Many models featured such luxury extras as walnut garnish molds, silk curtains, and vanity sets in the rear compartment.

While Pierce-Arrow hailed 1929 as a banner year, Packard had already had its eight on the market for five years. The latter was far ahead in engineering and design, and Pierce-Arrow would never catch up.

Nonetheless, riding the crest of a successful year, Pierce-Arrow tackled 1930 by expanding its line with the introduction of four wheelbase lengths—132, 134, 139, and 144 inches. The 132-inch Model C cars were powered by a new 340-cubic-inch engine, and the 144-inch Model A received a 385-cubic-inch motor. The other two models continued to be powered by the standard 366-cubic-inch engine.

Management then developed its first catalog custom body program for the 144-inch model, with coaches styled by Brunn,

While the Silver Arrow got most of the attention at the 1933 Chicago Century of Progress Exposition, there were many other advances by the company that year. This 1933 V12 LeBaron Convertible Sedan continued the company's propensity to attract an older market, but the real innovations were under the hood. Engineer Karl Wise created a new tappet-type hydraulic valve lifter, a mechanism that is now standard on virtually all cars.

Derham, Judkins, LeBaron, Dietrich, and Willoughby. The custom designs for its more lavish cars—the Town Landau, Convertible Sedans, and Convertible Roadsters—were virtual copies of competitors' models.

These moves by Pierce-Arrow represented a courageous attempt to break away from tradition, but it was too late; sales began to slide again. During the first quarter of 1930, Pierce-Arrow ranked a lowly twenty-eighth in national sales. The automaker was faced with a new generation of car buyers that was spoiled by the luxury and performance of the Packard eight and such dazzling newcomers as Duesenberg and Cadillac. By this time, Myron Forbes had resigned from the company and Studebaker's Albert Erskine had taken over as president.

In late 1931, Pierce-Arrow decided to enter the V12 market. Designed by Wise, the V12 came in two sizes. For the 1932 models, it came in 398 and 429 cubic inches. The following year, offerings were 429 and 462 cubic inches. By 1936, only the 462-cubic-inch engine was produced.

To gain publicity, Pierce-Arrow sent veteran test driver Ab Jenkins to the Bonneville Salt Flats, where he averaged 112.91 mph (180.7kph) over a twenty-four-hour period. In 1933, he went back, averaging 118 mph (188.8kph) over twenty-five hours. In its last run, Pierce-Arrow fitted its V12 with six carburetors and provided a streamlined body. It hit 127 mph (203.2kph) for twenty-four hours.

But Pierce's fortunes were hitting rock-bottom. Pierce had lost $3 million in 1932 with fewer than 5,000 units manufactured. Both Studebaker and Pierce had underestimated the severity of the Depression. Having overextended itself in financing Pierce, Studebaker declared bankruptcy in 1933. Albert Erskine committed suicide that same year.

A group of Buffalo businessmen purchased the company in 1933. Meanwhile, Roy Faulkner, who had become vice president for Pierce-Arrow in late 1932, was developing an entirely new car that would dazzle the motoring public. In 1933, he introduced the Silver Arrow, a radically designed vehicle promoted as the car that "gives you in 1933 the car of 1940."

Created by Philip Wright, designer of the Cord L-29 and former designer for coach builder Walter M. Murphy, the Silver Arrow was an anomaly among other Pierce products. Its styling did not influence other models.

Originally intended as a rear engine model, the Silver Arrow ended up a traditional vehicle. It featured an all-steel roof, flat sides

ABOVE: The Silver Arrow of 1934 and 1935 was a shadow of its former self. Most of Philip Wright's radical design of 1933 was junked in favor of a more conventional body. The fastback and the embarrassing V-shaped skylight remained. This 1935 model features the standard front fenders, exposed running boards, and narrow body. It still remains a handsome car, but it reflects Pierce-Arrow's reluctance to take chances. OPPOSITE: This is another conventionally-styled Silver Arrow, from 1934.

that covered concealed sidemounts and running boards. The doors were 1 foot thick, and their handles were recessed. The trademark Pierce radiator flowed easily with the rest of the aerodynamic body, which was placed on a 139-inch wheelbase and powered by a 462-cubic-inch, 175-horsepower V12 engine.

Only five Silver Arrows of this type were built, costing an astronomical $10,000 apiece. Pierce introduced another version in 1934, but it retained very little of the radical design of the five originals. The later version only kept the fastback styling and dual fender headlights. The Silver Arrows were offered as 8- and 12-cylinder models either on a 144- or 147-inch wheelbase.

Nothing, however, could save Pierce-Arrow from financial disaster. When it introduced the modestly priced Model 8 36A in March 1934, it was too late. In August of that year, Pierce-Arrow declared bankruptcy. For the first six months of the year, Pierce reported $681,000 in losses, $176,000 in July alone. The workforce, as many as 2,400 strong in 1930, was cut to six hundred.

Under a reorganization plan, the company name was changed from Pierce-Arrow Motor Car Company to Pierce-Arrow Motor Corporation. Prior to the bankruptcy, Pierce had hoped to sell 3,000 units as a break-even point. That figure was lowered to 1,770 units in 1935. But the cars still were not selling. Only 875 luxury Pierces were sold in 1935. Sales dropped again in 1936 to 787, then to an embarrassing 167 in 1937.

At one point, Pierce management had bragged that it was the only remaining independent that was devoted solely to building luxury cars. But this did not seem to matter. Nobody was buying. In 1937, the company ceased production. Unlike Cadillac—which was protected by GM—and the farsighted Packard, which read the market correctly and immediately built the 120, Pierce did not have the resources or the foresight necessary to survive.

When an impatient creditor demanded that Pierce liquidate to pay back a $200,000 loan, the company was forced into insolvency. Its assets amounted to only $40,000.

Coach Building

Building magnificent bodies for American and European automakers in the 1920s and 1930s was the swan song of most custom coach builders.

Many custom coach-building firms were founded in the nineteenth century and experienced success for many generations as carriage and wagon builders. With the advent of the automobile, coach builders found a new outlet for their creative designs, but their horse and carriage days were numbered.

What ultimately did in the custom coach builder was the stock market crash of 1929. Companies collapsed or were absorbed by competitors. Another major contributor to the downfall of the custom coach builder was the image of custom coaches themselves. The country was in economic devastation; bread lines stretched for blocks, and men who were once successful were reduced to selling apples on street corners. Families that lived in tent cities and struggled to feed themselves could not afford cars.

Although plenty of wealthy families remained to keep any number of coach builders in business, it was deemed poor taste to advertise one's wealth. The demand for luxury cars dwindled as the country sank further into an economic morass. When the United States entered World War II in 1941, the need and desire for the custom-built bodies continued to dwindle. Mass-produced cars in postwar America were cheaper. The wealthy became accustomed to owning high-priced cars that were just as pretty as cars from the previous generation, albeit inferior in quality.

Not all custom coach builders failed during the Depression, though. Fleetwood, for example, was protected under the huge umbrella of General Motors, and such builders as the Derham Body Company of Philadelphia found its niche in building limousines and later in automobile restoration.

Perhaps the best-known coach builder of its day was Brewster & Company, which was founded in 1810 at 52 Broad Street, New York, by James Brewster. The company constructed carriages for the city's elite for many generations before moving to a Broadway location that would later become Automobile Row.

In 1926, the Rolls-Royce Company of America purchased the company, making the new acquisition the principal builder for its American-made automobiles.

For a short period in the early twentieth century, Brewster manufactured its own 4-cylinder car—the Brewster—that was popular for city use. So it was no surprise that it began to construct town cars on modified Ford V8 chassis. These were not Fords and could not be purchased from a Ford dealer, but only directly from Brewster.

Brewster was recognized as early as 1906 for introducing a unique oil finish to its bodies. Lacquer was years away, and primitive technology prevented varnish paint jobs from lasting very long. Brewster developed a longer-lasting formula that did not contain varnish and did not dry completely. Its bright sheen enhanced the appearance of the car. Other builders attempted to copy the practice, but usually failed.

The company was also responsible for developing a windshield that reduced glare. Windshields of the day were vertical, and it was hard to see while driving in the city. Brewster produced at least two versions of a sloping windshield that reduced glare considerably, one of which had two separate panes sloping in opposite directions.

The Brewster family was no longer connected to the company after the acquisition by Rolls-Royce, but Henry Brewster re-emerged in 1927, forging a brief partnership with Harry Holbrook to design new bodies. But their venture lacked cash and did not survive long.

Another highly reputable New York company that fitted some of the most beautiful coaches to a variety of chassis was LeBaron Carrossiers, founded by Thomas L. Hibbard and Raymond H. Dietrich. The LeBaron firm provided design drawings to clients for a specific fee.

By 1923, Hibbard left the company and joined Howard Darrin in Paris to establish a new design business. Meanwhile, LeBaron was doing quite well. It won a contract with the Locomobile Company to design a new series of bodies. At that time, Locomobile was perhaps the most prestigious car in the United States. Custom-built either individually or in small lots, these cars sold at upward of $10,000. LeBaron designed the cars, and Blue Ribbon Body Company and Bridgeport Body Company built them.

In 1924, LeBaron merged with Bridgeport and became LeBaron Inc. One year later, Dietrich was lured by Edsel Ford to Detroit, where he established a reputation as an independent coach builder, designing Lincolns, Packards, and other luxury cars.

LeBaron continued to produce fine examples of what amounted to artwork on wheels including the 1923 Packard Convertible Sedan and the 1924 Wills Ste. Claire Town Cabriolet. In the early 1930s, LeBaron continued to build coaches for Packard, Marmon, Pierce-Arrow, and Stutz.

The Fleetwood Metal Body Company of Fleetwood, Pennsylvania, became a coach-building powerhouse when the Fisher brothers purchased the company in 1925 to become a division of the Fisher Body Company under the umbrella of General Motors. Founded in 1912 by H.C. Urich, Fleetwood remained a healthy company as automobiles became more commonplace in the decade before the Roaring Twenties.

Fleetwood moved the company headquarters to Detroit, where it became synonymous with General Motors, but some of its best work was as an indepen-

The *Locomobile*

Equal to the best imported cars in material, workmanship, and finish, but better adapted to American conditions...

A TRUE SIMPLEX. Our new catalog is fully illustrated and goes into details.

The Front-Vertical type of Gasolene Motor used exclusively....
Two Cylinder and Four Cylinder Models...

EASILY THE BEST BUILT CAR IN AMERICA.

Prices from $2000 upwards.

GASOLENE TOURING CAR
The *Locomobile* Company of America, Bridgeport, Conn.
BRANCHES:— NEW YORK, Broadway and 76th St.; PHILADELPHIA, 249 North Broad St.; CHICAGO, 1354 Michigan Ave.; BRIDGEPORT, Factory at Seaside Park; BOSTON, 15 Berkeley St.
Member Association of Licensed Automobile Manufacturers

LeBaron Inc. was truly one of the old-guard coach builders of New York, and remained influential in automotive design for more than three decades. An early client of LeBaron was Locomobile, a luxury car that predated many of the more famous marques.

dent. It manufactured bodies for Rolls-Royce, Stutz, and even Isotta-Fraschini.

Brunn & Company of Buffalo, New York, built its reputation on designing massive limousines and town cars, a reputation that was virtually unsurpassed in heavy construction by other coach builders. Founded by Herman Brunn, the company prided itself on the solid framework of its bodies. It often used bronze castings for body braces rather than the more typical wrought iron, which was heavier and less flexible.

A fine example of Brunn's work was a Pierce-Arrow Town Brougham built in 1929 for the shah of Iran. It was painted white with gold detailing. The exterior brightwork was gold-plated, and the shah's crest was displayed on each rear door. The interior hardware was made of 18-karat gold with the seats finished in woven white brocade with a laurel leaf motif.

Willoughby & Company was founded in Utica by Francis Willoughby and featured very conservative styling and quality workmanship.

Although the American coach builders had varied approaches to design, most constructed bodies the same way. Most wood for framework was hand-cut or bent into shape with steam to match the lines of the body. The wood used was usually northern white ash, although laminated oak was used for body sills. Body shops of the era often had a place set aside to age wood for up to a year so that it could acclimate to shop temperature and humidity.

The framework was joined together with glue and screwed joints. Wrought iron—occasionally cast bronze—was used at key points to strengthen openings such as doors. Most bodies were clothed in 14-gauge aluminum. Running boards for both European and American chassis were constructed from aged walnut or mahogany planks.

To satisfy a clientele accustomed to luxury, many coach builders paid more attention to the interior of an automobile than to the exterior. Since most cars were chauffeur-driven, coach builders were not always concerned with the driver's comfort and consequently built seats that forced the chauffeur to sit erect, since that was deemed proper posture. On cars other than those driven by a chauffeur, however, the physical characteristics of the driver were considered and the seat tailored to that driver's needs. Rear seats were constructed at a much more sloped angle, enabling the passengers to sink deeply into them. But those seats were not so deep as to bottom out on bumps.

The 1905 Locomobile provides an early example of LeBaron influences. While always regarded as one of the top coach builders, LeBaron never took chances with styling, maintaining the conservative look that attracted an older clientele. This was one reason why Raymond H. Dietrich left the company to start his own in Detroit.

Coach builders preferred to build seats the same way that fine furniture was made, with loose cushions, heavy padding, and separate pillows. Tufted upholstery was popular during the 1920s, and luxurious oil-tanned leather was usually the covering of choice for convertibles.

Most hardware was made of bronze or nickel-plated in bright or satin finish. Contrary to legend, custom-built interiors were not usually plated in gold. Cars built with solid gold or gold-plated hardware for such people as the shah of Iran were extremely rare. Actually, most interior trim was very conservative.

Vanity cases were provided with a wooden finish, and suede leather with gold trim was also popular. Virtually every case was equipped with a clock from Waltham, Jaeger, or Elgin. Typically, the woman's case was placed on the left since she entered the car first from the curb. A man's separate vanity case was placed on the right. This was reversed, naturally, for cars produced for British export. Traveling bars or writing desks were made of solid walnut or mahogany, as were the garnish moldings.

These items were standard equipment on most custom-built coaches. But many cars were built according to specific orders from customers. As a result, custom bodies built by the same coach builder on the same chassis often differ.

As World War II approached, these types of custom bodies were less popular with the motoring public. When postwar production resumed, there were very few chassis offered to custom coach builders, and an opulent era drew to a close. ❧

Stutz

MENTION STUTZ, AND BEARCAT INSTANTLY COMES TO MIND. INDEED, IT IS DIFFICULT TO THINK OF A STUTZ WITHOUT IMAGINING

a man wearing a duster and goggles behind the wheel of a Bearcat barreling down a dusty road at a high speed—or the Roaring

Twenties version with the driver wearing a raccoon coat and holding a flask of bathtub gin while cuddling a flapper.

Although the company survived for less than ten years during the classic car era, it managed to produce some of the finest

machines ever to grace the highway. Its underslung worm drive allowed for low, seductive

bodies, and its roofline on such models as the 1929–30 aluminum-bodied SV16 Monte

Carlo sedan was so low that it gave the appearance of a present-day chopped hot rod.

Perhaps most sensuous of all was the wooden-framed, padded leatherette-covered bodies

designed by custom coach builder Charles T. Weymann. These fabric bodies were light,

strong, and quite capable of soaking up road shock and noise. The Bearcat was easy to

repair, and the color of the car was impregnated in the lacquer-coated cloth. The color never

OPPOSITE: The 1928 Blackhawk Speedster was America's fastest production car, clocking 106.53 mph (171.4kph) at Daytona, a new stock car record. The Blackhawk moniker applied to all two- and four-passenger speedsters on the Model 8 BB chassis. This chassis was dicontinued in 1929. ABOVE: Predating the classic car era by ten years, this Stutz represents the rough-and-tumble era of racing on dirt roads. This fellow, with hat, goggles, duster, and a cigarette in his fingers, typified the masculine free-wheeling adventurous driver of a bygone age.

A stock Stutz at the Indianapolis 500 in May 1912 gets off to a quick start. Stutz entered thirty races that year and won twenty-five, with a minimal body that provided no comfort at all for the driver. Its chief rival at the time was the legendary Mercer.

faded. But Stutz's reputation as a dangerous performer on the open road and in the Indianapolis 500 scared off a lot of potential buyers. Morever, it was noisy at speeds of less than 50 mph (80kph). Nonetheless, the sexiness of a Stutz cannot be denied.

Harry Stutz had been making automobiles since 1898 from abandoned agricultural parts. Most of the cars he constructed through 1902 were strictly experimental or produced for some of the residents of his hometown of Dayton, Ohio. He had developed a single-cylinder gasoline engine but sold the rights to it in 1902 to another automaker. He went on to hold a series of automotive-related jobs in Indianapolis but did not stay long at any of them.

It was not until 1911 that Stutz succeeded in making a name for himself. He had founded his own business, Stutz Auto Parts Company, the previous year, and over the course of just five short weeks in 1911 he developed his own car. He immediately took it to Indianapolis where the now-famous 500-mile (800km) race was to have its inaugural running. His car, driven by Gil Anderson, came in eleventh—not a finish that prompted people to sit up and take notice, but Stutz managed to develop the advertising slogan "Car That Made Good in a Day."

What was amazing was that Stutz placed at all. It averaged 68 mph (108.8kph) with a 389-cubic-inch engine, far smaller than that of its competitors. A few weeks later, Harry Stutz entered into an agreement with Ideal Motor Car Company to manufacture his cars.

The Stutz was actually a compilation of parts from different manufacturers, and would remain so for many years. In its infancy, Stutz was powered by a T-head 50-horsepower Wisconsin 4-cylinder engine. In 1914, it offered a beefed-up 60-horsepower 6-cylinder engine to complement its 4-cylinder versions. During that year, the famous Bearcat was introduced as well.

The Bearcat was a true sports car, remarkably similar to the Mercer Raceabout, with a massive engine and minimal coachwork. It featured a hood, radiator, two seats, a fuel tank, and not much else. Comfort was not an option. Rumor had it that Stutz designed a stiff clutch specifically because he wanted to prevent women from operating the car.

The Bearcat won twenty-five of the thirty races it entered during that period. Stutz and Mercer had become merciless rivals and squared off often. Stutz usually came out on top.

Stutz's stock in the automotive industry rose with each model year. The company produced 266 cars in 1912, 759 in 1913, 649 in 1914, 1,079 in 1915, 1,535 in 1916, and 2,207 in 1917.

Increased sales translated into increased production, which made bigger facilities necessary. Harry Stutz also needed space to build his new T-head 16-valve engine. He went public in 1916, and Wall Street stock speculator Alan A. Ryan purchased a controlling interest. But Ryan was less interested in building cars than he was in challenging the old guard in the stock market with corporate raids, selling short, and attempting to boost the shares of Stutz. Stutz was disgusted with Ryan and resigned in 1919 to begin building a new automobile called the H.C.S. His new venture was a dismal failure, folding in less than two years.

Meanwhile, Ryan began to sink into a financial quagmire. In March 1920, he managed to boost a single share of Stutz Motor from $100 to $391. The following month, the New York Stock Exchange barred the company from trading. With his financial resources sapped by the constant free-for-all, Ryan was forced to declare bankruptcy in July 1922.

Bethlehem Steel magnate Charles M. Schwab, a good friend of Ryan, stepped in and paid Ryan $20 each for his 185,000 shares. Schwab was new to the luxury car market, but he was an art collector with a deep and abiding affection for fine living and lavish spending. The Stutz would be an excellent vehicle to exhibit his artistic tastes. He focused on transforming the Stutz into a more European car, and demanded that the company begin designing and building its own motors.

By this time, Stutz, which was earning a reputation as one of the best high-performance cars in the United States, rivaling Duesenberg, was pretty much a nonentity in the production sports and luxury car market. This status changed in 1925 when Schwab recruited Frederick E. Moskovics to assume leadership.

Racing enthusiast Moskovics, who had managed the Mercedes Vanderbilt Cup team, thought that the lessons of high-performance racing should be applied to production automobiles. A European-born student of race cars, he respected European technical innovations but was frustrated with the high costs and slow production that accompanied them. With Stutz, he had a chance to incorporate high performance into beautiful mass-produced cars.

Moskovics wanted to retain some of the car's racing image, but he also wanted to emphasize safety in order to draw in customers who were put off by the car's masculine image. In 1926, he shepherded in the Model AA, Safety Stutz, Vertical Eight—quite a mouthful. The idea was to accent safety and the company's new vertical-eight engine (not to be confused with Packard's straight-eight). With the vertical eight, Stutz left behind its rough-and-tumble image and stepped into the same field as Cord, Auburn, and, to a lesser extent, Duesenberg.

The Safety Stutz could go from 10 to 50 mph (16 to 80kph) in less than fifteen seconds, according to its sales literature. It made the most of its low center of gravity—as much as 5 inches lower than other cars with a conventional axle—which provided more stability while cornering. The vertical eight had a 287-cubic-inch engine, produced 92 horsepower at 3,200 rpm, and reached a top speed of 75 mph (120kph)—not spectacular by any means, but certainly enough to elevate its standing in the market.

Moskovics succeeded in producing a striking low-chassis vehicle that would handle well with the help of a low-profile Timken worm-drive differential. Timken differentials had been used on other cars, but were not up to luxury car standards because of profound noise problems. Timken conquered those problems and won a contract to have the differentials installed in Stutz products.

The Model AA chassis continued to be used through 1927, with an optional 145-inch wheelbase chassis becoming available late in 1926. With the new chassis, Stutz became the first automaker to provide a longer chassis, satisfying the demand of custom coach builders who wanted longer cars in order to develop more elaborate designs.

In 1928, Stutz contracted Charles T. Weymann and his company, Weymann American Body Company, to build fabric bodies, which created a stir at local shows. Weymann pioneered building bodies using lightweight wood substructures that were connected by hinged metal joints. The frame was then covered with leather or synthetic-leather fabric. Unlike in other luxury cars, the seats were attached directly to the chassis platform. This enabled the seats to flex, giving the driver and passengers added comfort.

But the public did not buy into it. Customers did not like the dull finish and the unconventional nature of enclosing a chassis in leather instead of steel. But the Weymann bodies were part of the mystique of the Stutz. With Moskovics' penchant for European styling, Stutz cars featured chic European monikers like Biarritz, Versailles, and Monte Carlo.

Stutz continued racing for a short period, winning the Stevens Trophy Cup in 1927 with a sedan. The Blackhawk speedster captured the AAA Stock Car Champion title the following year. The Blackhawk lost to Hispano-Suiza that year at Indy, but it

placed second in 1928 and fifth in 1929 at Le Mans. Its racing days, however, were temporarily over by the end of the decade as Moskovics focused on capturing a larger share of the luxury car market. But just as plans were laid, he resigned, leaving his right-hand man, Edgar S. Gorrell, in charge.

Gorrell decided not to enter the multicylinder engine fray in 1930 and 1931, but to perfect instead the vertical eight. Yet the public was bedazzled with 12- and 16-cylinder cars, and Stutz knew that it was at a disadvantage by not offering one. As a marketing ploy, Stutz renamed the vertical-eight the SV16 and the DV-32. The numbers denote the number of valves. An eager novice buyer probably leaped at the chance to see a 32-cylinder Stutz, only to find that it was actually 32 valves. But by that time, the buyer probably had been swayed by a sales pitch and was happy to purchase an 8-cylinder Stutz.

The SV16 vertical eight used a 322-cubic-inch engine that generated 115 braking horsepower. It still could not match the performance of most other luxury cars, but the company came out with a supercharger that boosted the horsepower to 143. The blow-er was mounted in front of the radiator and driven directly from the crankshaft. It was very noisy and caused some carburetion problems, but it generally performed well.

The DV-32 was quite a marvelous engine. It featured a dual overhead camshaft with four valves per cylinder. It produced 155 braking horsepower at 3,500 rpm and reached speeds of up to 100 mph (160kph). It also featured a four-speed Warner gearbox that was replaced in 1932 with an inferior Muncie three-speed gearbox.

The DV-32 was dubbed Bearcat, an old name but an entirely different kind of car than that of the teens. Stutz also introduced a Super Bearcat, with a special 116-inch wheelbase (as opposed to the Bearcat's 134.5-inch wheelbase) and fitted with the Weymann leatherette bodies. Less adventurous owners would later replace the leather with aluminum panels.

The DV-32 debuted at the New York Auto Show in late 1930, and in March 1931, prices were announced. The chassis alone cost $3,200, with thirty body styles offered. A full-bodied model cost anywhere from $3,995 to more than $5,000. In July 1931, Stutz saw a gross profit of $100,000. It wasn't much, but certainly much

Although not always particularly popular with the public, due to perceived maintenance problems, the Weymann body on such Stutzes as this 1930 model was truly unique. Charles T. Weymann wrapped leather or a synthetic-leather fabric around a light wood substructure to form the body. It was light and it cut down on road noise. When buyers balked, Weymann began wrapping leather around conventional bodies, but this too met with little success.

better than the dismal year of 1929. During this time, Stutz built upon the Cadillac concept of using drop-side body designs to conceal the chassis-frame side rails, which gave the car a lower appearance. Stutz also continued with its very low vertical windshield and rooflines, which complemented the high-riding and sweeping front-fender line.

At times, Stutz designs were showy, if not downright gaudy. Coach builder Rollston, for example, occasionally designed Stutz machines as if they were Duesenbergs. On its 1932 Stutz DV-32 phaeton, the color scheme consisted of light tones cut by molding that started at the radiator mascot and spilled over the rear portion of the hood to reflect the sweeping front fender line. The chrome trim for the molding then split off, with one line of trim sweeping back up across the cowl and another line flowing back between the front and rear cockpits. Wide whitewalls, stainless-steel wire wheels, and generous amounts of chrome finished off the extravagant creation. This was a far cry from Stutz's hellbent racing days, and showed how far the automaker had come in the luxury car market.

In the early 1930s, Stutz returned to racing. It entered the Indianapolis 500 in 1930 as a stock car and came in tenth. It also entered Le Mans, but never achieved the greatness it had attained in earlier runs. In September 1930, a Stutz driven by Cecil Bixby won the 140-mile (224km) Mexican road race between Nuevo Laredo and Monterey with an elapsed time of 1 hour, 56 minutes. Bixby averaged 70 mph (112kph) and beat the second-place finisher, a Studebaker Commander Eight, by two minutes.

Despite all its accomplishments and smart styling, Stutz continued to lose money. It reported a $315,000 loss in 1932, nearly half a million in 1933, and about $250,000 in 1934.

During the 1930s, fewer than 1,500 cars were produced. Only six cars were manufactured in 1934. The introduction of the modest 242-cubic-inch, 6-cylinder Blackhawk in 1929 had been Stutz's attempt to corner the luxury market, but sales were disappointing.

The company attempted to stay afloat by selling small panel delivery trucks called Pak-Age-Cars. But this strategy was not enough to save Stutz, which declared bankruptcy in April 1937. It reported $1.2 million in assets with only $733,000 in liabilities, but it could not pay its debts. When creditors could not agree on a reorganization plan, a judge ordered all assets liquidated.

Like Pierce-Arrow, Cord, and a handful of other specialty cars, Stutz did not go out with a bang, but rather with a whimper. In 1939, the firm was finally liquidated.

OPPOSITE: This 1929–30 Monte Carlo sedan was one of the most popular in the Stutz line. Its low roof-line gave the car an intimacy and sportiness not found on competitors' cars. The side windows were lengthened considerably to provide the driver and passengers better visibility. ABOVE: Declining to enter the multicylinder race, Stutz came up with the DV32. DV stood for dual intake and dual exhaust valves, thirty-two in all. Thanks to its designation as a DV32, this Stutz remained competitive with the V16 Cadillac. Pictured here is a 1933 Monte Carlo DV32. LEFT: The hood ornament on the Monte Carlo, with its solid neoclassical design, emphasized the dignity and reliability that Stutz wanted to convey with this car.

Part Two

United Kingdom

Aston Martin

WHENEVER AUTOMOTIVE ENTHUSIASTS DISCUSS THE GREATEST CARS EVER BUILT, THEY INVARIABLY POINT TO BUGATTI AND

Rolls-Royce as the European leading contenders and to Cadillac and Lincoln as the American ones. And sometime during this sub-

jective selection, the conversation always turns to Aston Martin.

When Lionel Martin began building his dream car, he wanted to combine Bugatti's perfection in handling and performance with

Rolls-Royce's attention to craftsmanship. Martin and Robert Bamford founded their marque in 1913. They had been selling Singer

cars but were unhappy with the quality and decided to manufacture their own high-quality sports car. Shortly after World War I, they

developed a car that was assembled from components constructed by outside auto suppliers. As a powerplant, they used the

Coventry-Simplex L-head 4-cylinder with a 1,389-cc displacement. They fit it into a small 1908 Isotta-Fraschini racing chassis and

named it "The Hybrid."

Martin and Bamford used the Hybrid as a test vehicle, driving throughout England, making adjustments here and there. This

vehicle proved to be a prototype for later models.

Martin's cars were a long way from being sold to the public. Martin was more interested in racing, but he had hoped to mass-

OPPOSITE: Up until 1926, the Aston Martin was actually a product of Bamford and Martin, a partnership of Robert Bamford and Lionel Martin. This 1924 model, with a 1½-liter, sixteen-valve engine, was one of the last cars built before Aston Martin went into hiatus and was reorganized in 1926. The 1½-liter model did exceptionally well at Brooklands track, averaging 86.21 mph (137.9kph).

LEFT: While Aston Martin resumed production in late 1926, few cars reached private owners until the introduction of the International four-seater in 1930. It could reach 80 mph (128kph), and it handled twisting British roads remarkably well. Unique to the International were the full-cycle wings attached at the rear of the 14-inch alloy brake drums on all four wheels. ABOVE: An enduring quality of the Aston Martin International is the absence of streamling or any attempt at styling. The nose, busy and somewhat cluttered, appears to have just left the racing track, exactly the effect that designer Harry Bertelli had hoped to achieve. OPPOSITE: Following the success of the International, the Le Mans debuted at the 1931 Olympia Motor Show. This 1932 model is similar to one purchased by Jimmy Nervo, a popular English comedian who appeared regularly at the London Palladium during the 1930s. Race car driver A.C. Bertelli captured the Biennial Cup at Le Mans in 1932 with this model. Note the elaborate external exhaust system.

produce his creations for public consumption.

Despite the success of the Hybrid prototype, a new car was not finished until 1921. It was called the Aston Martin—Martin, of course, for its founder, and Aston in honor of the Aston-Clinton Hill climb in which Martin's Singers had done particularly well during competition.

The car was a modest three-seater, eventually powered by a 1,486 cc 4-cylinder engine, which enabled the car to race in the 1,500-cc class. The Aston Martin had a nondetachable head, a sin-

gle carburetor, and a three-bearing crankshaft. The chassis was fitted with two-wheel brakes, although later models would be equipped with four-wheel brakes. The chassis was underslung at the rear with semi-elliptic springs at the four corners. The steering was surprisingly quick and nimble.

Compared to other high-performance cars of the day, the Aston Martin chassis was modestly priced at about $3,000. Nevertheless, the company suffered financially between 1921 and 1927, despite a cash infusion from Count Louis Zborowski, a wealthy sports car enthusiast. Virtually nothing was produced in 1925, and a paltry fifty cars rolled off the line the following year.

The company was reorganized in 1926 as Aston Martin Ltd. and was based in Feltham, Middlesex, a suburb of London. Augustus Cesare Bertelli and W. S. Renwick were brought in to lead the design staff.

In 1927, Bertelli designed a whole new car that sported many firsts for Aston Martin. The new engine featured a cylinder head shaped somewhat like a cone or pitched roof with the spark plug at its peak. The valves were located on each side of the plug, and a single chain-driven overhead camshaft moved the valves through the rockers.

A specialty of the Bertelli design was an oil tank in front of the radiator that was part of the dry sump lubrication system. It helped keep the oil cool since it was located out front as engine oil circulated through the engine and back to the tank. Another feature, found on virtually all sports cars today, was a four-speed, close-ratio gearbox that was not integral to the engine, but moved back toward the cockpit to allow for a short gear lever and enhance a short throw.

Bertelli produced about fifteen of these models in 1927 and 1928, but they were extremely heavy. Both Martin and Bertelli were eager to sell these sports cars to the public, but they still had to solve the weight problem and make the cars more comfortable for routine driving.

Bertelli entered the 1928 Le Mans with two teams driving a pair of Aston Martins. Both cars did well as they averaged over 60 mph (96kph) for about thirty laps. But Bertelli's car broke a rear axle at Lap 31, and the second car fell out because of a broken gearbox, with six hours to go in the race. Bertelli had to take some weight off the Aston Martin's chassis by drilling and replacing brass and steel with light alloys.

Bertelli also had to contend with other nuisances. These models were sprung like wagons and every bump in the road was felt by the driver and passenger. The old-fashioned crashbox had had its day, and if these cars were to be sold to the public, easier shifting was paramount.

The "International" debuted in 1930 to meet this demand. Powered by a 1,495-cc, 4-cylinder overhead cam engine with a 69.3 × 99mm bore and stroke, the model was a four-seater capable of hitting 80 mph (128kph)—not a great speed but fine for the motoring public. The car was somewhat primitive compared to American sports cars at the time and was something akin to a pre–World War I Stutz.

But the International was one of the prettiest sports cars on the road in 1930. It sported motorcycle fenders attached to the rear backing plates, which turned with the wheels. Its angular hood featured many louvers, plated external exhaust pipes, and knock-off wire wheels.

As 1933 approached, R. Gordon Sutherland took over the financially troubled Aston Martin Ltd. He began to make some major design changes that ultimately would lead to a more comfortable sports car, abandoning the rough-and-tumble crashbox sports driving of the 1920s. He eliminated the heavy torque tube and introduced spiral bevel gears instead of the traditional—but not always reliable—rear-axle worm drive.

The Mark II debuted in 1934 with a boosted compression ratio of 7.5 to 1. With its near-twin, the Ulster, the Mark II defined the best of Bertelli-based designs. Ulster was a much more powerful machine than the Mark II, reaching speeds of 100 (160kph) mph and breaking the 1.5-liter record at Le Mans in 1935. The record stood until 1950.

But with the Mark II and the Ulster came sacrifices. These Aston Martins now featured more stampings and fewer hand-finished castings. The marque was beginning to lose its precision in what appeared to be a concession to a new generation of drivers that did not have the patience to wrestle with a crash-type gearbox. This was evident with the introduction in 1936 of a 2-liter Aston Martin with no motorcycle fenders and sump lubrication and equipped with a synchromesh gearbox.

But these later Aston Martins should not be dismissed as the work of a marque that had sold out. These cars typified the thoroughbred sports car design with low lines, cut-down doors, racing windscreens, headlights protected by screens, and fine, driver-friendly instrument panels. Indeed, these cars established the foundation for today's sports cars.

ABOVE: This Mark II Saloon debuted in 1934 and with a 1500cc engine and 7.5-to-1 compression ratio that generated 75 horsepower, very high for a 1500cc engine. These models came equipped with the Hotchkiss drive, which replaced the old torque tube drive. OPPOSITE: The sister of the Mark II, the 1934 Ulster could hit speeds of up to 100 mph (160kph). The Ulster broke the Le Mans 1.5-liter record in 1935 and held on to that record until 1950. But the Ulster also marked the beginning of the end for the old-fashioned crash-box type of driving, as Aston Martin used fewer hand-finished castings, reducing the car's hand-built distinction.

Bentley

"**W**E WERE IN RACING NOT FOR THE GLORY AND HEROICS, BUT STRICTLY FOR BUSINESS," WALTER OWEN BENTLEY ONCE said. The Bentley spent so much time on the track that it will be associated forever with some of the greatest European racing achievements, including its glory years at Le Mans in the 1920s.

W. O. Bentley saw an opportunity to put his automobiles in the public eye through racing, but his focus had always been luxury passenger cars. He was less concerned with weight-saving devices that would increase speed and enhance performance than he was with building massive, perfectly built machines powered by engines capable of pulling brutes of any size.

The endurance of the Bentley is evident in the often-told story of the 1927 twenty-four-hour Le Mans road race in which two 3-liter Bentleys and one 4.5-liter Bentley competed for the top prize, only to find a French Schneider spun out across the road at White House Corner at 9:30 at night. Leslie Cunningham was driving the 4.5-liter model when he turned the corner at 80 mph (128kph) to find the Schneider in his way. He ditched his car, smashing it to pieces. George Duller added his 3-liter Bentley to the heap moments later. Following Duller

OPPOSITE: The 4.5-liter Bentley was the car of choice for Ian Fleming's James Bond in his early books. Fleming hoped to astonish his readers with something that stood out in a crowd. This 1929 4.5-liter Touring Bentley was probably what Fleming had in mind. The 4.5-liter was the pride of Bentley at Le Mans in the late 1920s and in 1930. In 1929, the four Bentleys that started crossed the finish line in 1–2–3–4 order at Le Mans. ABOVE: The 1926 3-liter four-cylinder Red Label was a workhorse at Le Mans. During its six-year lifespan, about 1,600 models were turned out. The street models generated 88 horsepower at 3,500 rpm. The specially tuned Le Mans competitors attained nearly 95 horsepower.

was S.C.H. Davis in the other 3-liter Bentley. Davis slammed on his brakes and attempted to maneuver his Bentley so that only the rear of the car would be damaged.

Davis' Old Number 7—but racing as Number 3 for this race—sustained serious damage that would have spelled doom for any other automobile. The Bentley had a badly bent front axle, a broken wheel, cracked steering-arm joint, broken headlights, and smashed fenders.

But the car managed to continue. After it limped back to the pit, a flashlight was attached to the roof and whatever could be fixed with baling wire and chewing gum received attention. Davis took the car back out on the track until midnight, when codriver J. D. Benjafield took over.

Benjafield hated driving at night and was faced with the added ordeal of navigating through rain. The Bentley handled poorly, and all right turns were driven blind because the right headlight was out. But by early morning, the Bentley was second to an Aries. Benjafield pressed the Aries by punching the gas pedal. The Aries blew its engine, and the Bentley hurtled across the finish line for a first-place finish. Not only did the Bentley capture first, but the performance confirmed its reputation as one of the most reliable cars in Great Britain and Europe.

Despite such successes—both in automobile performance and public relations—Bentley's company was never on firm financial ground during its twelve-year existence. Even the birth of the Bentley in 1919 was difficult at best.

For one thing, Bentley's first love was not the automobile but locomotives. Like Frederick Royce, Bentley served an apprenticeship in the dirty shops of the Great Northern Railway. He also served a year as a fireman, shoveling vast amounts of coal into old high-wheeled Atlantic locomotives.

When he founded his automobile company, he had nothing resembling a factory or a showroom. His only offering in 1919 was a 3-liter prototype that debuted at the Motor Show at Olympia. His first car was not sold until 1921, as he spent considerable time perfecting the prototype.

He also was faced with ruthless competition. Other automakers circulated rumors that the Bentley was a compilation of parts from other automobiles.

Although every piece on the Bentley was indeed original, except the electrical system, the rumors hurt him.

The public also could not have cared less about his most notable engineering achievement—the aluminum piston. Pistons of the day were made of cast iron or light steel and disintegrated at high revolutions. Bentley, however, developed a light aluminum piston that not only performed well at higher engine speeds but had a higher compression, thanks to better dispersal of heat.

But Bentley eventually won over consumers primarily through word of mouth and later through a string of phenomenal successes at Le Mans. Production began to pick up, with 204 Bentleys manufactured in 1923. And 403 3-liter models were produced in 1924, which proved to be the largest production year of any Bentley. Victories at Le Mans in 1924 and in 1927 through 1930 were unsurpassed by any competitor until Ferrari and Jaguar came along after World War II.

OPPOSITE: The 1930 Bentley Speed Six is a larger version of the famous "Big Six." The Speed Six had a compression ratio of 5.3-to-1 for the street and 5.8-to-1 for Le Mans. It could could top 100mph (160kph) and finished first in the 1929 Le Mans. ABOVE: Driver S.C.H. Davis navigates his 3-liter Bentley during the last four laps at the 1927 Le Mans following the infamous White House Corner crash. His smashed right front fender and headlights and badly bent front axle didn't prevent "Old Number 7" from racing to a dramatic first-place finish.

The 3-liter models would become Bentley's most popular automobile during the company's brief life. The 3-liter, 4-cylinder engine had an 80-mm bore and a 149-mm stroke that gave a high torque at low revs. The camshaft was driven by a vertical shaft at the front of the engine. Two magnetos supplied spark to two spark plugs per cylinder. The engine generated 65 braking horsepower at 2,500 rpm, enabling the car to reach 90 mph (144 kph).

Known as the "Red Label" model because of the color of its radiator badge, this car enjoyed a six-year run between 1921 and 1927. By the end of the production run, later Green Label and Blue Label models were developing 88 braking horsepower at 3,500 rpm. About 1,600 3-liter models—including the Green Label and Blue Label versions—were produced, with as many as 500 of these Bentleys surviving today.

Bentley, meanwhile, was busy producing bigger versions. In 1926, a 6.5-liter model—the Big Six—debuted. It was driven with a system of connecting rods and eccentrics from the crankshaft. The Speed Six, a larger version of the Big Six, was introduced in 1929 with a compression ratio of 5.3 to 1 as standard and a 5.8 to 1 ratio in the racing version, which could reach 100 mph (160kph).

A dramatic innovation from Bentley came in 1927 with the 4.5-liter model. This was a 4-cylinder version of the Big Six. Many of its parts were interchangeable with the 6-cylinder models and are now considered more desirable by collectors. About fifty of the 4.5-liter models were supercharged, developing 182 horsepower and capable of 105 mph (168kph). The 4.5-liter model was manufactured in time to compete at the 1927 Le Mans. It was one of three Bentleys to be wrecked at White House Corner.

The manufacturing of the 4.5-liter supercharged model was ill-advised. Designed by Sir Henry Birkin, the supercharger was seen by W. O. Bentley as a perversion of the original model. Yet he authorized its construction at a time when the company could not afford such a luxury. By this point, Bentley was verging on bankruptcy. But Woolf Barnato, a popular Bentley driver and son of Barney Barnato, a South African diamond king, infused a large sum of cash to keep the company going for a while.

By 1929, Bentley was beginning to show a modest profit, thanks to the Big Six models. From a mar-

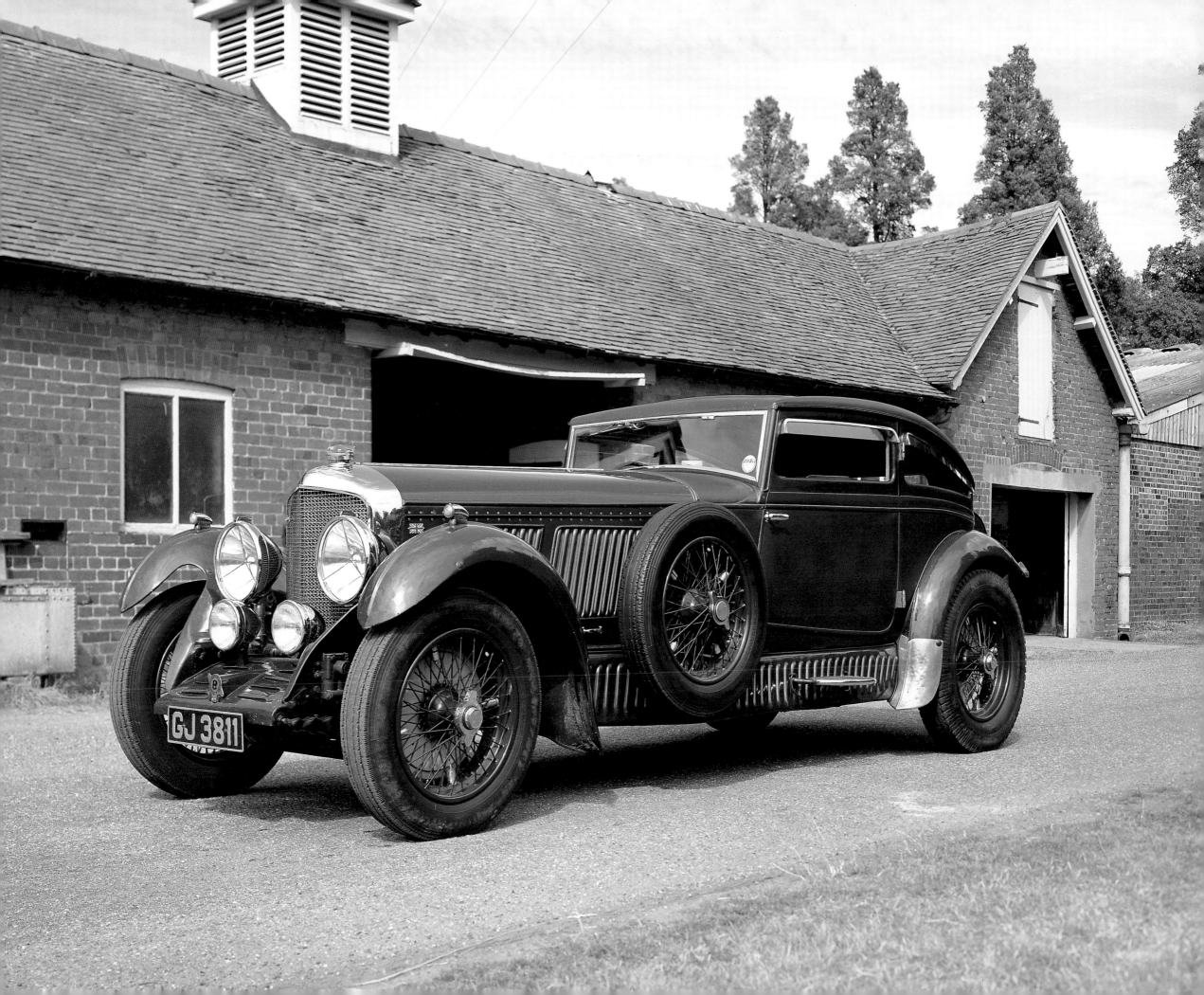

For 1931, the 8-liter, this one a 1931 Tourer, replaced the 6.5-liter model, and it became Bentley's most popular model. Its introduction stunned the automotive press, for it clearly was not a sporting car, but more for the social elite. The 8-liter turned out to be Bentley's swan song, as the company failed that year.

keting standpoint, it helped that the Bentley team wrapped up the top four places at Le Mans that year.

Production for the 6.5-liter models was 129 cars for 1929 and 126 for 1930. The 4.5-liter models did better for the same period: 260 and 138, respectively.

Although Bentley enjoyed modest success in its short history, the company was still running low on cash. In an effort to boost sales, Bentley came out with the 8-liter model in December 1930. Designed not as a sports car but as a high-end luxury model with speed,

the car came with either a 144- or 156-inch wheelbase. Its steering was effortless, and its speeds were astonishing for the time. In 1956, Forrest Lycett clocked his 8-liter model on the Herentals-Antwerp express highway in Belgium at 141.7 mph (226.7kph).

The 8-liter model was designed to attract the very wealthy, but its timing could not have been worse. The chassis cost $9,000, and there were not many people during the worldwide Depression who were able to spend so much money. Only about a hundred 8-liter models were manufactured.

Seven months after the debut of the 8-liter, the London Life Assurance Company sought a receiver for Bentley Motors after Woolf Barnato, the principal stockholder of Bentley, refused to meet his mortgages. Napier Motors attempted to acquire Bentley, but Rolls-Royce stepped in at the last moment and purchased the assets of the company. Subsequent Bentleys produced by Rolls-Royce were little more than Rolls-Royces with Bentley badges and radiator grilles. Total production of the true Bentleys, produced between 1919 and 1931, was 3,061.

ABOVE: The winged mascot of a 1930 Bentley Speed Six, suggesting a balanced combination of speed and rugged power. LEFT: Only one hundred 8-liter models were built before Bentley's collapse. Part of the reason for the low numbers was the $9,000 price tag for the chassis. This model, a 1931 convertible coupe, was built by an American company, Murphy, of Pasadena, California.

Rolls-Royce

ETTORE BUGATTI, CREATOR OF THE FAMED BUGATTI ROADSTERS, COMPLAINED THAT HE COULD NEVER UNDERSTAND WHY ROLLS-

Royce was considered the epitome of luxury and high performance.

Isotta-Fraschini and Hispano-Suiza matched Rolls-Royce point for point in luxury and engineering. There were American cars that were faster and just as reliable. The Rolls-Royce was not a particularly stylish car, reflecting the image of a conservative, well-mannered Englishman. And Rolls-Royce management disapproved of ostentatious designs by zealous coach builders.

What set Rolls-Royce apart from its competitors was its craftsmanship. That is not to say that it was the best car ever built. The Cadillac was perhaps the best-built American car of the era, thanks to Henry Leland's preoccupation with precision machining.

Rolls-Royce's engineers, also fanatically devoted to precision-built automobiles, suggested that owners return their cars to the maker when they reached 50,000 miles (80,000km) so that the

OPPOSITE: The reputation of the Rolls-Royce was built on this 1907 40/50 Silver Ghost. It was the first car to be virtually noiseless and smokeless. It was so quiet that a sign was posted in the yard of the factory stating "Look Out for Silent Cars." It was said that the Silver Ghost forgave bad drivers and stimulated good ones. RIGHT: There was no mistaking a Rolls-Royce when it traveled down the road, thanks in part to the double-R badge stamped on the radiator. The 40/50 was named "Silver" for the color of the first racing car and "Ghost" because it was so quiet.

cars could be dismantled for inspection. A two-hundred-page instruction booklet accompanied each automobile and was expected to be followed to the letter by either the owner or chauffeur. The automaker also offered to send an inspector to the owner's residence to give the car its annual checkup. And if that was not enough, Rolls-Royce offered to teach either the owner or chauffeur techniques in driving and maintenance at its own automotive school.

Englishmen of the early twentieth century expected nothing less. These services set Rolls-Royce apart from the automobiles manufactured in Detroit, but none of this was a publicity gimmick. Dragging Rolls-Royce owners into the plant to allow a crew to break down a car at an ungodly cost was not exactly a public relations man's dream.

Frederick Henry Royce once described building his cars as "sewing" parts together. The Silver Ghost, for example, used dozens of tiny bolts that almost touched one another to fasten the torque tube; other manufacturers used only eight, ten, or twelve bolts. This was a method that Henry Ford abhorred as too complicated, expensive, and unnecessary, but it typified Rolls-Royce's "sewing" process. The automaker might produce only five cars in a single week, and it was not uncommon to have inspectors return all five to the plant to have them rebuilt because a flaw was discovered somewhere.

Rolls-Royce aimed for perfection. And this preoccupation led to one of Rolls-Royce's main goals: silence.

In an era when cars used primitive external oilers that often created a noisy, oily, smoky mess, Rolls-Royce was a welcome relief. Experimenting with manifolds and mufflers and meticulously fitting and machining parts, Rolls developed a hollow crankshaft that was fed with oil from a pump. With the timing drive to the camshaft and ignition through gears instead of chains, the Rolls-Royce was a silent marvel.

The philosophy of supreme craftsmanship was the result of an unlikely alliance between the Honorable Charles Stewart Rolls

TOP LEFT: This 1911 40/50 Silver Ghost typified the style of the Edwardian era of England—stiff, upright, and stuffy. While the designs of most cars of the era were holdovers from the horse-drawn carriage of the previous century, it took Rolls-Royce longer than most to consider style an integral part of the car. BOTTOM LEFT: A rare and somewhat radical design for the Rolls-Royce is seen on this 1914 Silver Ghost with wooden boattail. The fenders are strictly old style, but the rakish windshield adds a nice touch.

and Frederick Henry Royce. Rolls, an entrepreneur who operated several motor car agencies, was born into wealth and had an adventurous spirit. Royce, a perfectionist born into poverty, worked as a newspaper hawker, a mechanic's apprentice, and an electrician.

Like Henry Leland, founder of Cadillac and Lincoln, Royce learned the value of precision machining. As a boy, he worked in the tough and grimy Great Northern Railway shops during a time when children workers were little more than slaves. An apprenticeship was a long, hard road. And a worker was not considered a journeyman fitter until he could file a square on the end of a brass rod and a square hole in a brass sheet to enable the rod to fit into any of four positions perfectly. All this was done by hand.

Royce purchased his first car in 1903—a French Decauville, then considered one of the premier European vehicles. But Royce did not like the car and thought that he could build a better one. By this time, he was a partner in a small electrical equipment business. When the company hit lean economic times, he turned his attention to automobiles.

Charles Rolls, on the other hand, had owned cars since 1894, when he bought a Peugeot. He was co-owner of an automobile agency in London that specialized in luxury cars. Rolls and Royce met in 1904, and together they developed a high-performance automobile unsurpassed by any European competitor. With Rolls' marketing skill and Royce's flawless workmanship, they formed Rolls-Royce. Their first effort was a 4-cylinder, 20-horsepower machine. Forty were manufactured in 1905 and 1906.

In 1906, the pair won the Tourist Trophy Race, beating their nearest competitor by twenty-seven minutes. But Rolls knew that mechanical perfection alone would not sell cars, so he sought publicity at every opportunity. He would supply Rolls-Royces to British royalty, including the Prince of Wales, in an effort to show that his cars belonged in an elite class. And it was soon apparent why the wealthy flocked to these automobiles: they were the only cars of the time in which two people could carry on a conversation in normal tones while driving on the highway. The Rolls was truly a comfortable car and instantly elevated the station of any owner.

Perhaps Royce's greatest triumph came in 1906 when he created the 40/50 6-cylinder car, later known as the Silver Ghost. It was named "Silver" for the color of the first racing version and "Ghost" because of its silence.

There was nothing particularly innovative about this car, but its detailed perfection was remarkable and remains unmatched even

This odd-looking 1924 Rolls-Royce was obviously heavily influenced by the World War I era biplanes, with its tapered rear end and the passenger seat located directly behind the diver. Body styling was executed by Labourdette of Paris.

by today's cars. Its chassis was similar to the earlier versions, but the engine was all new. It was powered by a 454-cubic-inch L-head 6-cylinder side-valve motor that had two blocks of three cast-iron cylinders with integral heads and side-by-side valves. The crankcase was made of aluminum alloy and carried seven main bearings. As in the first engines developed by Royce, the timing drive to camshaft and ignition was by gears, not chains. The helical timing gears were made of phosphor bronze and nickel steel, and ground and polished by hand. The crankshaft was ground to an accuracy of .00025 inches on its bearing surfaces. It was then polished to remove the microscopic scratches left by the grinder. The car was a smokeless, noise-less wonder.

A rare car that made any person an expert driver on the road, it was easy to handle on tight city streets and a pleasure cruiser on the open rural road.

The Silver Ghost was Rolls-Royce's sole offering between 1906 and 1925. At the beginning, the automaker produced only four cars a week, hitting its peak in later years at seven cars each week. Total production output was 6,173.

Royce was a cautious and conserv-ative man. Though he tinkered with his creation a bit, making a few minor changes, it was the same basic car during its nineteen-year life span. A 4-speed gearbox replaced the 3-speed one in 1913. Electric lights and starter did not debut until 1919. In late 1923, it adopted an Hispano-Suiza–type 4-wheel brake system.

By 1922, Rolls-Royce produced its first "baby" model, a smaller version of the Silver Ghost with less power under the hood. This was not an attempt by Rolls-Royce, though, to capture buyers with less money. After all, these "babies" cost as much as $8,000. Rather, Rolls recognized that drivers living in cities did not want huge cars to navigate the narrow streets. Few of these cars were shipped to the United States, since road conditions there were so

ABOVE: Coach builder Brewster of New York was especially fond of designing the Ascot Phaeton and Riviera Town Car. This Phantom I Ascot Phaeton epitomizes chic. Unlike Duesenberg and other luxury automakers, Rolls-Royce eschewed flashy adorn-ments for its moving palaces. OPPOSITE: Considered by some to be the last great luxury car, the Phantom III debuted in 1936. It was the first Rolls-Royce series built after the death of Frederic Royce in 1933. This Phantom III Sedan de Ville has a 7.34-liter V12 engine, generating 165 horsepower at 3,000 rpm and able to reach 100 mph (160kph).

much more favorable than in Great Britain, and consequently there was less need for a smaller Rolls. But they were popular in England, especially among women drivers who did not possess the upper-body strength required to handle a larger, more physically demanding model.

The first baby Rolls-Royce was powered by a 20-horsepower engine, whereas the larger cars were rated between 40 and 50 horsepower. Throughout the 1920s and 1930s, power in the smaller cars was increased to 20/25 and 25/30 (because the British govern-ment taxed cars by horsepower, English car horsepowers varied in ratings). Despite the increase, power in these models proved woe-fully inadequate, with a maximum speed of only 60 mph (96kph).

Styling on the Silver Ghost line was stodgy—upright with massive fend-ers and an ungainly belt line, which dipped too much at the doors. The car featured the famous red Rolls-Royce badge that appeared on every model between 1906 and 1933. The lettering was changed to black after Royce's death in 1934. The appearance of the Silver Ghost was more similar to a horse-drawn carriage than to a masterly crafted specimen that represented the wealthy.

The directors at Rolls-Royce were aware that they were lagging behind their American counterparts with respect to styling. Cadillac and Lincoln produced some very beautiful styles, and in Europe, Hispano-Suiza's designs continued to reign supreme. Other luxury cars, like the Isotta-Fraschini and the Bentley, were regarded as superior in design as well. Rolls-Royce's answer to these competitors came at the London Auto Show in late 1925, with the introduction of the Phantom I.

The chassis of the Phantom I was not too different from that of the Ghost, with its torque-tube drive and long can-tilever rear springs. Four-wheel brakes had become standard. The engine, how-ever, was new.

The stroke was increased to 5½ inches, and the bore dropped slightly to 4¼ inches, providing an 8 percent increase in displace-ment and 33 percent more power. This actually boosted the horse-power to about 100, but Rolls-Royce is an unusually secret compa-ny, and has never been comfortable releasing such data, so that fig-ure is an estimate.

The standard L-head valve setup was changed to a pushrod-operated overhead-valve arrangement. Rolls-Royce toyed with a 12-cylinder V-type engine and an in-line 8-cylinder, but ultimately rejected them in favor of the 6-cylinder version. A supercharger was also tested, but was dismissed as too noisy, too complicated, and too extravagant.

The body of this Phantom III was designed by Figoni et Falaschi, and displays the sportiness Rolls-Royce could achieve even with a four-door pillarless model. The Phantom III came with independent front suspension, but enthusiasts often argue over whether the Phantom III was better engineered than its predecessors. While handling and reliability may not have matched earlier versions, it was considerably faster than them.

This 1929 Wraith Sedanca with body styling by J. Gurney Nutting is a dramatic departure from earlier versions. This vehicle was Rolls-Royce's foray into the modern era. And 1929 marked the first year that chassis were welded, abandoning the famous sewing process that used fitted tapered bolts in reamed holes. Only 491 Wraiths were made before World War II.

By this time, Rolls-Royce was operating its Springfield, Massachusetts, plant as Rolls-Royce of America, Inc. In theory, the automaker's American-made cars were not significantly different from the British models, but several distinct characteristics were found in the Springfield cars.

The Springfield models had, of course, lefthand-drive and a 3-speed gearbox; the English ones had a 4-speed transmission. The American version also dispensed with the magneto found on British models.

The Phantom I was not the fastest car of its day but was capable of hitting 80 mph (128kpm), keeping pace with Detroit-built cars. Besides, high-speed driving in England was not really an option for drivers because of the 20 mph (32kph) speed limit. Nevertheless, power did become a factor when the engine was required to move the massive bodies produced by such coach builders as Brewster of New York, who created fine designs in the Riviera Town Car and Ascot Tourer.

In all, more than 2,200 Phantom chassis were manufactured at the Derby plant between 1925 and 1929. Between 1926 and 1931, 1,240 were produced at the Springfield facility.

The Phantom II was introduced in 1929 with basically the same engine as its precursor, although its power was increased slightly to about 125 horsepower. The chassis was all new. To correct some of the poor cornering and handling of earlier versions that had torque-tube drive, the frame was stiffened significantly. The outdated cantilever rear springs, long a Rolls trademark, were replaced with half-elliptics.

One year later, the sporty "Continental Touring" model was introduced on a 144-inch wheelbase. This car was capable of hitting speeds of more than 90 mph (144kph), thanks to flatter springs, a slightly higher rear-axle ratio, and a higher compression ratio of 5.25 to 1. Later models were equipped with close-ratio gearboxes and adjustable shock absorbers for better handling.

The Phantom II was the last true Rolls-Royce. Frederick Royce died in 1934, and the Phantom III, which debuted in the fall of 1935, continued the tradition of fine workmanship and perfection. The Phantom III was radically different from any previous Rolls-Royce offering. The 6-cylinder engine was scrapped in favor of a very complicated V12 with hydraulic valve lifters, which were replaced two years later by solid tappets. There were early complaints that the V12 was not as reliable as the old 6-cylinder engines, but mounted on a chassis with a 150.5-inch wheelbase, this tremendously large car could move from a standstill to 60 mph (96kph), in about sixteen seconds and could hit speeds of 100 mph (106kph), on the open road.

The new models also came equipped with independent front suspension. Each front wheel had a shock absorber mounted inside a horizontally mounted coil spring.

By the end of the 1930s, the Phantom III moved over for another Rolls-Royce venture: the Wraith. A scaled-down version of the Phantom III, the Wraith had a chassis that marked a dramatic departure from previous models. The Derby plant had always produced chassis that were held together with fitted, tapered bolts in reamed holes, but this chassis was welded. Only 491 25/30 models were manufactured before World War II broke out in 1939, when Rolls-Royce began supplying the Royal Air Force with Merlin aero-engines. The first postwar model to debut in 1946 was the Silver Wraith.

Rolls-Royce continues to deliver superb driving machines virtually unmatched by any other luxury automaker. Its basic design has remained unchanged for decades.

Today's automobiles owe a debt of gratitude to Rolls-Royce for pioneering the luxury of silence and superb craftmanship. It's no wonder that the marque continues to carry the slogan "The Best Car in the World."

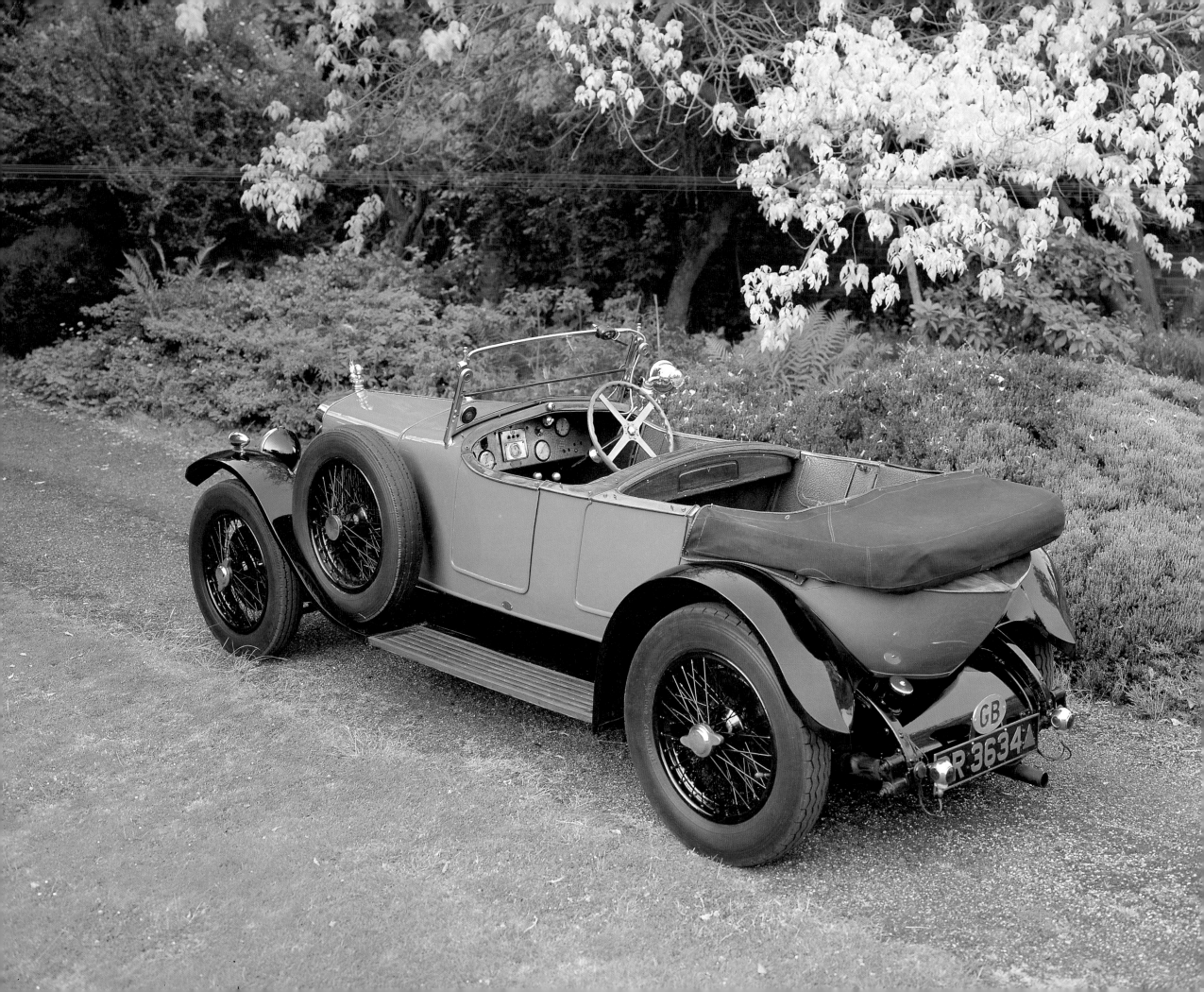

Part Three

France

Bugatti

BEFORE ETTORE BUGATTI DIED IN **1947** AT THE AGE OF SIXTY-SIX, HE PRODUCED ABOUT **9,500** AUTOMOBILES, EACH ONE A WORK

of art. Of these, the remaining 1,200 are definitely museum pieces.

Bugatti generally ignored the conventional wisdom of automobile building. Priding himself on his independence, he was rarely

influenced by other engine designers. He remained faithful to some of his early theories and princi-

ples long after other automakers had abandoned them as obsolete.

A man of great drive, Bugatti possessed more than a thousand patents and spent many sleepless

nights working on projects other than his famed automobiles. He built aircraft engines, gasoline-

powered locomotive engines, children's cars, four-wheel-drive vehicles, and even marine engines.

He was also arrogant. When a customer once complained that his Type 55 was difficult to start

in cold weather, Bugatti replied, "If you can afford a Type 55 Bugatti, surely you can afford a heated

garage!" Bugatti had an aristocratic attitude although he often lived hand-to-mouth and sometimes

OPPOSITE: This 1926 Bugatti Type 23 Brescia is a detuned version of the much better performing Type 22, yet it still remained one of the best cars of the day. The chassis for this car was lengthened to make it more practical for touring purposes. The car was produced from 1923 to 1926. RIGHT: Clearly one of the best cars ever to be driven, either in the United States or Europe, this Bugatti Royale is instantly recognizable for its mascot, egg-shaped radiator, and distinctive Bugatti label.

ABOVE: The Type 23 Brescia is one of the smallest Bugattis ever produced, with a very short 93 inch wheelbase chassis. There were two versions, the full Brescia and the modified Brescia. The full version was the fastest hill climber in England from 1923 to 1926. OPPOSITE TOP: The Type 40 served as a replacement for the modified Brescia in an effort to attract the not-so-wealthy. The four-cylinder 1500cc engine differed little from the Type 37 model, with the exception that it had a coil instead of magneto ignition and a lower compression ratio. It was built from 1926 to 1930. This one is a 1930 Type 40 GP. OPPOSITE BOTTOM: Ettore Bugatti's son, Jean, was highly involved in designing this 1937 Type 57 Atalante Coupe. It was a temperamental beast, but with the chassis selling for as low as $2,860, it was a good choice for buyers with expensive tastes but modest means. The body on this Atalante coupe is aluminum, and it came with a horseshoe radiator instead of the traditional egg-shaped version. The Type 57 was built between 1934 and 1940.

paid his employees with chassis that they could sell themselves. He loved art and appreciated beauty in motion.

If ever there was an automobile that personified its maker, it was the Bugatti. Ettore Isidore Arco Bugatti was born in 1881 in Italy, but lived nearly all his life in France.

The son of a cabinetmaker and silversmith, Bugatti was urged by his family to become a sculptor. But his brother, Rembrandt, was better at sculpting, and Bugatti did not want to be in his shadow. So at the age of sixteen, he turned to the automobile and never looked back.

In 1898, Bugatti designed and constructed his own 4-cylinder automobile and raced it in several French races, winning at least three. With his third car, a compact vehicle of original design, he won the 1901 International Sport Exhibition in Milan.

These successes caught the attention of de Dietrich, a railway equipment manufacturer that wanted to expand its enterprise to automobiles. The company gave Bugatti a generous contract with exclusive rights on the Italian market, which allowed him to sell cars that were trademarked de Dietrich–Bugatti cars. His reputation as an innovative designer was established within two years after building five different models for the company.

Bugatti continued to serve apprenticeships through 1909 but was never under anyone's tutelage for very long. He served as technical manager for Deutz Gas Motor Works from 1906 to 1909 and built his first car bearing his own name. It was a very light compact automobile with an overhead valve, 4-cylinder engine that bore a remarkable resemblance to the Type FE Isotta-Fraschini. The car went on to win its class in the 1908 Grand Prix des Voiturettes in Dieppe.

In 1909, Bugatti discovered an old dye plant in Molsheim. After cleaning it up and purchasing the necessary equipment, he opened his car manufacturing plant in early 1910. He hired a small crew, whose ranks swelled to about sixty-five in 1911. Five cars were produced in 1910, and that number jumped dramatically to seventy-five in 1911.

Bugatti's first effort in his new plant was the Type 13. This 4-cylinder car featured the now instantly recognizable red-and-white oval nameplate on the top half of the egg-shaped radiator grille. Half-elliptic springs were used at the corners. The engine had two vertical valves for each cylinder. Four brass plugs were installed into each side of the aluminum cam cover.

The Type 13 put Bugatti on the map as a serious competitor in racing, starting with the 1911 Le Mans when Ernest Friderich

raced it to win its class and earn second place overall. Although the winning trend continued for many years, there was an interruption in production during World War I. The Molsheim plant was located in an operational zone, and Bugatti moved to Paris for the duration. (The region in which the plant was situated was taken from Germany at the end of the war and came under French rule.) Although he produced no cars during this time, he continued to register many industrial patents until production resumed after the war ended.

The first postwar car to debut was the Type 22, a modified Type 13. Five of the Type 22s had been hidden at the onset of the war in 1914 and were pulled out of storage to capture first place at Le Mans in 1920. The engine had a 1,400cc displacement, but was boosted to 1,500 for the 1921 model. It came with sixteen valves, two spark plugs per cylinder, and two Zenith carburetors. Four of the Type 22s raced at the 1921 Italian Voiturette Grand Prix near Brescia and finished 1-2-3-4. Born of this magnificent showing was the Type 23 "Full Brescia," which was raced throughout Italy.

Bugatti experienced tremendous success in racing. Between 1924 and 1927, Bugattis won 1,851 races. Ettore Bugatti did not have much use for publicity in those days, letting his cars' racing records speak for themselves. He immediately took advantage of his on-track successes and expanded his factory to a thousand employees by the mid-1920s. The British, in particular, seized the Bugatti as the car of choice for its superb handling on winding, narrow country roads.

Because there are so few surviving examples of the vehicles Bugatti produced in the 1920s and 1930s, it is impossible to give each one thorough discussion. But a number of them stood out as his greatest achievements.

In 1924, he introduced his most elegant race car, the Type 35. With a body designed by his son, Jean Bugatti, the Type 35 Grand Prix rivaled the works of the finest Italian and French coach builders of the day. It is now considered the most famous racing Bugatti.

Ettore introduced his new creation in grand style at the 1924 Le Mans in Lyons. He invited nearly fifty people to the event, providing them with tents that contained running water, refrigerators, showers, and electricity. It was a display that suited the Grand Prix.

The most remarkable change to this model was the cast-aluminum wheels, which had broad spokes cast into the rims. The spokes were designed to deflect air against the brake drums for cooling. When the wheels were removed, the brake drums came with them, making brake repairs easy.

The engine was a straight-eight (straight-eights debuted in 1922 with the Type 30), 1,991cc affair, with three valves per cylinder and five ball-and-roller bearings. The connecting rods were not fitted with bearing caps but were of lightweight, one-piece, H-section forgings.

A Type 35A, more commonly known as an Artificial or Imitation 35, was offered for sale to the motoring public. A 35B was supercharged with a three-lobe Roots blower mounted beside the cylinder block and enlarged to a 2,262cc displacement with five ball-and-roller bearings. The 35C, which debuted in 1927, also was supercharged, clocking a maximum speed of 127 mph (203.2kph).

The Type 40 debuted in 1926 as a replacement for the Brescia Modifie. It appealed to those customers who hungered for a Bugatti, but did not have the money to purchase one. It sold for $1,770 in England. The engine was nearly identical to that of the Type 37 with its 4-cylinder, 1,496cc "square-cut" style. However, the Type 40 used a coil instead of the traditional magneto ignition and lower compression ratio. In terms of top speed, the Type 40 never matched its predecessor, reaching only 75 mph while the Type 35 could hit 100 mph (160kph).

Bugatti's most beautiful—yet eccentric—creation was the Royale Type 41, which was completed in early 1927. This huge automobile was more powerful than any Bugatti previously built. Unquestionably the finest example of Bugatti's workmanship and design, it was reminiscent of a grand style seen only in the luxury coaches of locomotives or ocean liners.

The prototype Royale, built on a 180-inch wheelbase, was Bugatti's personal car. The straight-eight engine had a bore and stroke of 125mm × 150mm and a mind-boggling displacement of 14,725cc. The engine block and cylinder head were a single-unit aluminum casting weighing a whopping 238 pounds (107.1kg). The water jackets in the block were drawn around each cylinder for maximum cooling. The pistons were also made of aluminum, and the connecting rods were forged steel. All this generated 300 braking horsepower at 1,700 rpm. Overall, the car was surprisingly light, weighing only 5,600 pounds (2,520kg).

The chassis was fitted with a Packard Eight touring body, then replaced with a small nondescript coupe, then a large four-

ABOVE: Jean Bugatti died in 1939 while testing a new car, but he lived to see the Type 57 evolve into one of the most powerful and stylish machines ever put out by the Bugatti plant. This is a 1939 Type 57 Van Vooren Cabriolet. OPPOSITE: Unquestionably the finest car Bugatti ever built, and perhaps the finest ever built by anybody, the Type 41 Royale made its debut as a prototype in early 1927. It was huge and powerful and without a doubt the most lovingly constructed vehicle on the market. The engine alone measured four feet, seven inches, and the crankshaft weighed a whopping 225 pounds. The engine output was 300 braking horsepower at 1,700 rpm.

door sedan. Finally, Bugatti installed a fine Weymann two-door coupe body.

Bugatti was so pleased with this prototype that he ordered twenty-five chassis, a large number given his low annual output. The production models, however, were small, with a 170-inch wheelbase and a 12,763cc engine. Only ten were produced between 1927 and 1933, largely because of the $30,000 price tag, which was unreasonable—even for the very rich—during the worst years of the Depression.

Each Royale Type 41 was unique. One version, a roadster by Binder, was commissioned by Armand Esders of Paris, who asked that his model not be equipped with lights, since he never drove after dark. In 1930, Joseph Fuchs, a German physician, had Munich coach builder Ludwig Weinberger construct a cabriolet. The car was moved to the United States in 1937 and was rescued from a New York junkyard six years later. Ultimately, it was restored. One Royale was even smuggled underground by the French Resistance to keep it out of German hands. Bugatti's personal Royale was badly damaged after he wrecked it on a French highway. The car was rescued and rebuilt as a coupe de ville by Henri Binder.

Between 1934 and 1940, Bugatti produced what was perhaps his most successful car, the Type 57. With a low $2,860 price tag, it was a temperamental vehicle, but a love-hate relationship evolved and endured. The Tourer Type 57 debuted in 1934, and the Type 57S and 57T came out the following year. The 57S (S for sport) was placed on a shortened wheelbase of 117.5 inches, compared to the touring models of 130 inches. The sport model also had a higher compression ratio, increased from 6.2 to 8.3, and a displacement of 3,257cc. Coupled with the changed valve timing, the sport model had 190 braking horsepower at 5,500 rpm and could hit 125 mph (200kph), while the 130 horsepower Tourer 57 had a top speed of 95 mph (152kph). The 57SC was supercharged and boasted 220 horsepower. When it was raced by Robert Benoist on the Montlhery Autodrome in France, it hit 135 mph (216kph) in 1936. The 57S version placed first at Le Mans in 1939.

These accomplishments, however, were interrupted in 1940 by World War II. Bugatti would never fully recover.

On August 11, 1939, Ettore's son, Jean, heir to the Bugatti firm, died. Although he was not permitted to race his father's cars, he was killed while testing one on a road outside of Molsheim. Upon rounding a turn at a high speed, he encountered a drunken man in the middle of the roadway. He swerved to avoid hitting him and crashed.

When the Germans occupied France, they purchased the Bugatti factory at their own price. After the war, the plant was occupied by Canadian and American troops. The Canadians accidentally started a fire, which heavily damaged the contents and structures. To make matters worse, the Americans removed machine tools and lost many Bugatti records.

France, Bugatti's adopted country, seized the plant as enemy property because Bugatti retained Italian citizenship. The automaker sued and lost at first, but won on appeal. However, the ordeal took its toll on the old man. As the appeal concluded in May 1947, he went home a sick man. He died on August 21, 1947.

The firm limped along for a while, producing the 3,257cc engine-powered Touring Type 101 and supercharged 101C in 1951 and Grand Prix Type 251 with a 2,487cc engine. But Bugatti never could reclaim its past glory.

Delage

LOUIS **D**ELAGE WAS NOT A WELL-LIKED MAN.

He drove his son from his automotive business and, during a temper tantrum, fired his cousin, the company's head engineer. He had expensive tastes and tortured his long-suffering wife by pursuing other women. And he ran his enterprise with an iron fist.

An accomplished engineer, Louis Delage surrounded himself with the best automotive men in the business. His engineering standards for three decades were superior, and he viewed each creation out of his factory as an art object. As the Lincoln was to Edsel Ford and the Bugatti to Ettore Bugatti, the Delage was, over its thirty-year life, an extension of Louis Delage's personality. It spoke of refined elegance and occasional excess, and it tried so hard to match the legendary Hispano-Suiza that Delage's 1924 Grand Luxe model nearly bankrupted the company. Whatever Delage's shortcomings were, few enthusiasts today would disagree that it was the Delage and Hispano-Suiza—not Delahaye or the Talbot-Lago—that confirmed France's reputation as home to some of the finest automotive builders in the world.

Born in Cognac, France, in 1874, Delage graduated from the École des Arts et Metiers at Angers in 1893 with an engineering degree. He initially sought a career in the railroad business and secured a minor position at a station in Bordeaux. But the primitive

OPPOSITE: The first Delage production car to appear on English roads was the Type DI, featuring a two-liter, four-cylinder engine and four-wheel brakes. By 1925, a more powerful version, the Type DIS, debuted, and was produced through 1928. The DISS, or DI Super Sport, appeared in 1926. In this photo is a 1925 Delage DIS. An estimated 938 variations of the DI were built.

technology of automobiles lured him to the industry that would give him an opportunity to use his creativity, which was being stifled in railroading.

At the turn of the century, he did a series of minor jobs as a consulting engineer. But by 1903, he had established solid credentials that enabled him to get a job as chief draftsman for Peugeot, then a small but thriving automobile company. His tenure at Peugeot lasted two years, long enough to give him the confidence and experience he needed in order to obtain the financial backing to establish his own company, Delage & Cie., in 1905.

From Peugeot, Delage took with him Augustin Legros, who was six years his junior and eager to expand his horizons. Like Delage, Legros possessed an engineering degree. Joining the new company as its designer, Legros would remain with Delage for the life of the company.

The pair struggled along, and by the end of 1905 they had completed two prototypes, the 1,059cc Type A and the 496cc Type B. When the cars were shown at the Salon de l'Automobile de Paris, the two men quickly discovered that all the displayed vehicles had engines that were either too big or too small to be practical for the motoring public. They quickly came up with their third model, the 697cc de Dion, which was an immediate success.

Like many automakers of the day, Delage believed that automotive racing was a marketing tool necessary to stimulate sales. He entered two cars in the grueling weeklong Coupe des Voiturettes de l'Auto. One car was wrecked, but the other finished second to a Sizaire et Naudin, while the highly regarded Peugeots limped in at third and fourth place.

The subsequent publicity brought fame to the early Delages, and by 1907, the little automotive plant had expanded. In October 1907, Delage entered the Coupe des Voiturettes and finished a respectable seventh out of fifty-six contenders. He attracted the attention of a tool-manufacturing firm, which became a silent partner providing much-needed capital. Henri Davene de Roberval, president of the board of directors for the tooling company, became a major stockholder and would remain so until Delage ended its operations in 1935.

In contrast to most automakers of the day, which assembled their cars from previously manufactured parts, Delage designed and constructed its own frames and most of its hardware. By 1909, the company was manufacturing 50 percent of its own engines.

By 1912, Louis Delage had expanded his factory again, this time purchasing 11 acres at Courbevoie, which bordered the

When this 1911 Delage 12-horsepower Type TR appeared on the market, it was the eve of a major transformation for the automaker. Delage had always specialized in manufacturing light cars with engines ranging from a single cylinder to four. But the Delage plant at Lavellois was not adequate, so eleven acres at Courbevoie were purchased to expand the operation and better serve the Delage clientele.

Hispano-Suiza property. Delage's obsession with outdoing his neighbor would prove ruinous.

Before World War I, Delage was highly successful, specializing in small, light cars powered by engines equipped with one to four cylinders and not larger than 2.1 liters. He sold these cars at competitive prices and managed to make them very stylish.

During these early years, Delage's reputation in the French automotive empire was secure. During the war, however, faulty munitions were manufactured at the plant, and Delage's production manager was sentenced to five years in prison on criminal charges.

Although Delage himself escaped scandal, he was never regarded in the same way by the French government. He was denied admission to the Legion d'Honneur, which was awarded to nearly every man of his stature in the country.

After the war, Delage concentrated on producing large cars and in October 1919, it introduced the Type CO. The car was powered by a 6-cylinder long-stroke, 4.5-liter, side-valve engine. A new CO debuted in 1921 with an overhead-valve engine that topped 80 mph (96kph). Thanks to a seller's market in postwar France and the automobiles' large size, Delages became wildly popular. Although

Louis Delage made lots of money during the war, it was the CO that enabled him to purchase a new town house, move his offices to more stately headquarters, and build showrooms in the best locations in France.

Aside from the early introduction of four-wheel brakes in 1919, there were not many engineering innovations during this period. But the product produced by Delage could not be topped by any other manufacturer. With the fine finish applied to the entire chassis and engine, his cars were considered among the most glamorous of their day.

Delage continued to prosper. The CO and later CO2 were followed by the Type DE and the later DI series, which sported an overhead-valve 2.1-liter engine.

Delage went public with his firm in 1923 and saw its capital increase from 1 million francs to 25 million francs. But all was not well. Delage's son, Pierre, who suffered under his father's iron will for many years, quit the business in a huff after an especially bitter argument. He worked in various other automobile ventures for six years before returning to Dad.

During this time, Delage continued to chafe under the lofty reputation of Hispano-Suiza. Determined to humble his neighbor at any cost, he recruited Maurice Sainturat, a designer of considerable reputation, to develop a stunning offering for the automotive show in Paris in October 1924.

Sainturat demanded and received total independence from the rest of Delage's engineering staff and embarked on a project that ultimately proved to be Delage's folly: he created the Grand Luxe, a thing of rare beauty. The 6-cylinder engine had a bore and stroke of 95 × 140mm with a 5,954cc displacement, which generated 100 braking horsepower. It was equipped with unusual (for its day) features such as overhead valves operated by an overhead camshaft, dual ignition, and four-wheel brakes. It also was equipped with pump cooling. It was offered with either a 143.9-inch wheelbase or a 153.1-inch wheelbase. The chassis sold for $5,340, and the price of the total car was about $8,250.

Although Delage had Hispano-Suiza in mind when he had the Grand Luxe built, the car actually was more akin to the Rolls-Royce Silver Ghost in terms of luxury and performance. It was listed as a 40/50 Delage in France, but England listed the car as a Delage 34-horsepower Type GL.

Two hundred Grand Luxes were manufactured, with 180 designated as touring models. The 143.9-inch wheelbase models were marketed for England and Germany.

ABOVE: By 1923 Delage decided it was time to challenge the existing speed records in Europe. During that year he developed a 10.5-liter V12 engine and had Rene Thomas race it at Arpajon. On July 6, 1924, Thomas raced a 1924 Delage V12 at 143.24 mph (230.47kph). While it did well during those early months, the V12 wasn't always successful. Design changes were made in the chassis and the engine was supercharged, to produce 190 horsepower at 7,000 rpm. It then went on to win the Grand Prix de France. Above is a 1924 Delage V12 Grand Prix. RIGHT: The spartan but very functional cockpit of the V12.

This was to be Delage's perfect contribution to the luxury market. But the cost of assembling two hundred cars over a two-year period was draining on the company. Moreover, the Grand Luxe's engine was extremely fragile on account of a sliding joint in the vertical shaft driving the single overhead camshaft. Requiring frequent repair, it was the engine's weak link. The Grand Luxe faded away just two years after its debut because, despite its luxury, buyers feared its undependability.

During this fiasco, Delage fired his cousin Planchon, who headed the standard engineering department. This left the design of the Type DI to others, who produced a car that was not up to the usual standards of a Delage, though it sold well enough to see the company through the 1920s.

But the DI and the Grand Luxe gave way to a much more practical and celebrated automobile, the Type D8. The D8 was perhaps Delage's finest example of automobile construction. Its chassis came in lengths ranging from 130- to 143-inch wheelbases. The D8S (sport chassis) had a 122- to 130-inch wheelbase. These chassis were destined to support some of the most exotic coachwork ever to grace four wheels. Figoni et Falaschi produced two- and four-door saloons and coupes for the English market during the early years of the model.

The car was powered by a pushrod straight-eight engine with overhead valves. It had a bore and stroke of 77 × 109mm with a 4,050cc displacement and a crankshaft that carried five main bearings. Top speed with these engines exceeded 100 mph (160kph), quite a feat in 1929.

The D8 chassis sold for $3,125, and the car's price was $4,400. Between 1929 and 1933, only ninety-nine sport chassis were built, and 1,902 D8s were manufactured.

By the end of the D8's production run in 1933, the company was suffering. The unrealistic Grand Luxe and Delage's entry into the 1927 Grand Prix World Championship severely crippled the company's financial resources. Although the D8 took some of the Hispano-Suiza market, the worldwide Depression spelled doom for the project from the start. The D8, along with Delage's DS and D6 models, was too expensive and could not be moved off the showroom floors.

In 1932, Delage obtained a loan of 25 million francs. It also introduced the modest 6-cylinder 2,001cc D6 11, which sat on a short 122- or 129.3-inch wheelbase.

But the new funds quickly dried up, and it was becoming increasingly difficult to meet expenses. By 1935, the company had been absorbed by Delahaye after Peugeot rejected Delage's proposal that it take over the entire distribution and sales organization of his company.

Delahaye, never much competition on the racing circuit, owed a debt of gratitude to Delage for its sudden racing successes after acquiring the company. Following the acquisition, Delahaye unceremoniously pensioned off Louis Delage.

The Delage D8 continued to live under the Delahaye regime, but as a 6-cylinder model—merely a shadow of its former self. The Delage badge disappeared completely in 1954 when Delahaye was purchased outright by Hotchkiss.

Louis Delage died on December 14, 1947. His longtime friend and designer, Arthur Legros, died on March 12, 1953.

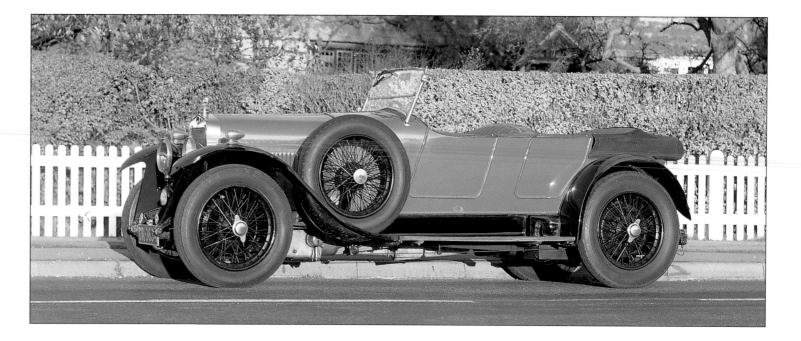

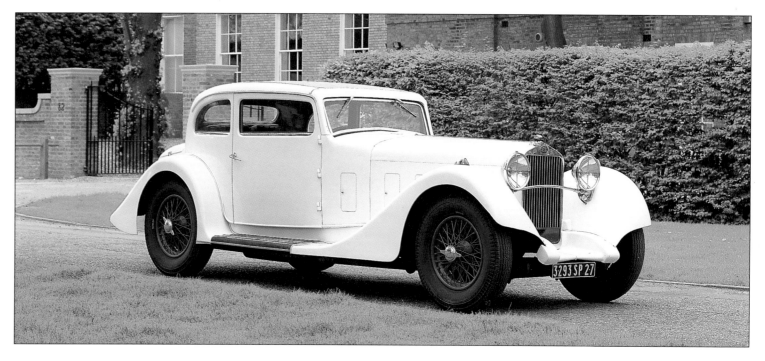

TOP: Another variation of the DI Series is this 1926 Delage, which proved to be the workhorse of the company through the middle and late 1920s. ABOVE: The roof line on this 1933 Delage D8S by coach builder Letourneur et Marchand is strikingly similar to the Stutz models made at the same time on the other side of the Atlantic Ocean. The D8S models, produced between 1930 and 1936, are probably the most attractive cars of the classic car area. OPPOSITE: No longer a true Delage, the 1937 D8 120 was the last of the "Delahaye" Delages, models manufactured by Delahaye but carrying the Delage label. The performance of these models was less than satisfactory. Although the engine was enlarged to 4.7 liters, more than 1,000 pounds (450kg) was added to the curbside weight, making it far heavier than the earlier D8S models. Maximum speed reached only 90 mph (144kph) despite a 140 horsepower output. This Delage is identified as a 1938 D8 120 model with coach work by Letourneur et Marchand.

Delahaye

ALTHOUGH **D**ELAHAYE BEGAN PRODUCING LUXURY CARS AT THE BEGINNING OF THE CLASSIC CAR ERA, IT DID NOT EMERGE AS A true competitor in the field until 1935, when it acquired Delage.

Although Delahaye was a significant racing presence before 1900, the company had many other ventures, and racing—long the most desirable marketing tool of auto manufacturers of the era—took a backseat to more lucrative ventures during the first two decades of the twentieth century. Gas and steam engines, fire trucks, heavy- and light-duty trucks, and inboard boat engines were all produced at the Delahaye factory. Marine engines became such a popular item for the company that Delahaye ruled in speedboat racing events between 1904 and 1914. In 1904, it captured first place thirty-four times. The following year, Delahaye broke the world's speedboat record at Monaco.

The marque began with Emile Delahaye, a chief engineer with Franco-Belgian, which manufactured railway rolling stock. Delahaye left Franco-Belgian, and in 1890 acquired a machine

OPPOSITE: The Delahaye 135 achieved unprecedented success in the mid-1930s, breaking seven world records and eleven international records with an average of 110 mph (176kph). By 1936 the 135 became more streamlined and racier. Delahayes performed well at the 1936 French Grand Prix, coming in behind the first place Bugatti in second, third, fourth, and fifth place. This is a 1937 Delahaye 135M Cabriolet with coach work by Guilloie. ABOVE: An early 8-horsepower Delahaye automobile in 1895. This vehicle was belt-driven, with a radiator constructed of bent tubing. A Delahaye similar to this one competed in the 1,000-mile (1,600km) Paris-Marsilles-Paris race in 1896. The Delahaye was a frontrunner in automotive racing, particularly during its early years.

This 1936 Delahaye Type 135 typifies the models that tore up the race track, breaking numerous speed records. In 1936, two 6-cylinder engines were provided in the Delahaye, with the competition version built to attain more than 110 mph (176kph). But Delahaye's track successes didn't occur consistently until it acquired Delage in 1935.

shop that produced gas and kerosene engines. This modest concern blossomed toward the end of the decade, when Delahaye observed that Gottlieb Daimler and Karl Benz were achieving great celebrity with their continuing automotive innovations. Delahaye had recognized that automobiles, not steam engines, were the future.

Delahaye was intrigued with practical, lightweight German cars with water-cooled engines. In 1895, he produced a belt-driven car with a radiator constructed of bent tubing not unlike the early Benz models. He immediately entered two of these versions— equipped with pneumatic tires—in the 1896 1,000-mile (1,600km) Paris–Marseilles–Paris road race. Delahaye drove one car and Ernest Archdeacon took the other. Archdeacon finished fourth and Delahaye sixth.

Delahaye continued to produce belt-driven engines. He moved his plant from Tours to Paris and began looking for a factory manager. Charles Weiffenbach, affectionately known as Monsieur Charles, was a suitable choice for Delahaye, and he remained with the company until its demise in 1954. By this time, Delahaye had joined forces with Leon Desmarais and Georges Morane, who helped secure the company's financial backing.

Monsieur Charles was the heart and soul of the company. He was conservative and stubborn but took on a tremendous workload and was largely responsible for the company's producing so many different lines of transportation equipment.

For a three-year period in the late 1800s, Delahaye continued to produce cars at a rapid pace. These cars were 1- and 2-cylinder models that boosted between 7.5 and 9 horsepower. The wheelbase was 70.9 inches, and steering was controlled with a straight steering column that had bicycle-type handlebars. Six hundred of these machines were manufactured.

Delahaye retired in 1901, leaving Desmarais, Morane, and Monsieur Charles to continue building the Delahaye empire. In 1902, with the debut of the Type 10B, the belt-driven engine was abandoned for chain-driven engines. Placed on an 83-inch wheelbase, the 10B sported a 12/14-horsepower, 2-cylinder engine. The first big car, the Type 13B, debuted in 1903, setting the stage for a number of low-priced, mid-sized models.

At the same time, Delahaye was fast becoming the leader in the manufacture of heavy trucks. Their fire trucks became the equipment of choice for many local departments in France. Shortly before World War I, the company also introduced light trucks, which became popular for newspaper deliveries and with the French post office.

duced a new low-silhouette body with a pointed radiator that spruced up the car.

The first true postwar Delahaye debuted in 1920 with the Type 84. Powered by a 4-cylinder engine and coupled with a lighter chassis, the Type 84 was quick and agile. It remained a standard for all Delahaye cars until 1928.

The year 1920 also marked the debut of Delahaye's first true luxury car, the Type 82. The 82 was powered by a 6-cylinder engine that boasted 20/30 horsepower.

But by the late 1920s, Delahaye was coming into hard times. Low-priced, mass-produced cars based on the Henry Ford concept were becoming increasingly popular in France. Delahaye clung to more distinctive designs with an emphasis on quality, but the demand for elegance was rapidly shrinking. Moreover, a drop in sales of heavy trucks alarmed Delahaye management.

Looking for help, Delahaye joined Chenard & Walcker and the F.A.R. Tractor Company in an effort to establish the French version of General Motors. But this venture failed. Many years earlier, Monsieur Charles had attempted to convince French automakers of the advantages of standardizing parts and sharing supplies to mass-produce cars. But independent French automakers could not accept such restrictions to competition and they soon began to split off into various factions, producing boldly distinctive cars.

Faced with the Depression and a failing financial empire, Monsieur Charles realized that he would have to abandon his traditionally heavy chassis of the Teens and 1920s and produce lighter and faster models. He introduced the 6-cylinder Superluxe model with independent front suspension and a new stylish body. A 4-cylinder version also was produced. In 1934, a new Type 135 was built with a stock 18-horsepower engine. It broke seven world records and eleven international records with an average speed of 110 mph (176kph). The racing victories were the first significant wins for Delahaye in nearly thirty years.

The 135 continued to win a string of European road races. In 1935, Delahaye acquired Delage and added to its fleet of cars 4-, 6-, 8-, and 12-cylinder cars. Many of these continued to race under the Delage badge.

At the 1936 French Grand Prix, Delahayes finished second, third, fourth, and fifth. First place was awarded to Bugatti. The 1936 Delahayes were powered by a 3.5-liter 160-horsepower engine equipped with three carburetors.

Delahaye's shining moment arrived in 1937 with the Prix du Million, a race that would award 1 million francs (about $80,000)

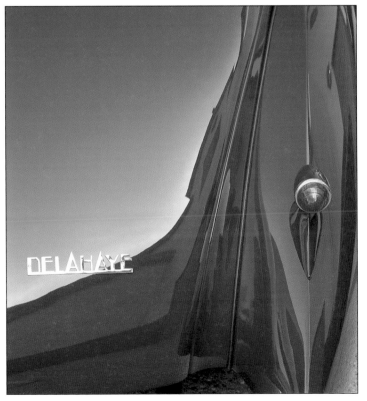

ABOVE: A Delahaye 135 passes a burning Hudson in the 1936 French Grand Prix. Bugatti garnered the top spot, but four Delahayes captured spots two through five. The Delahaye reached its peak in establishing speed records in the mid-1930s. LEFT: Guilloie, along with other coach builders including Franay, Figoni et Falaschi, Pourtout, and Saoutchik, designed some truly startling bodies for Delahaye over the years. This is a 1937 Delahaye 135M Cabriolet by Guilloie.

At the onset of World War I, the French government turned to Delahaye to develop a fleet of heavy-duty machines to contribute to the war effort. Delahaye came up with the 3½-ton Delahaye 59, a 4-cylinder, 30-horsepower vehicle, which outperformed Aries, Berliet, and Renault as the most reliable vehicle in combat service. (In fact, when German troops occupied France in 1940 and seized all modern trucks, the World War I–vintage Delahaye 59s—more than twenty years old at the time—were able to keep France's commerce going.)

In 1919, the company returned to manufacturing passenger cars, producing the Type 64N, which was not much different from prewar models. But noted coach builder Merville et Garnier pro-

OPPOSITE: Delahaye continued to rack up victories on the track in 1938. This 1938 Delahaye 135M Convertible Coupe is one of the last examples of prewar styling before World War II began the following year. By this time the 12-cylinder engine was offered to the public in low-slung bodies. TOP LEFT: Another example of the famed Delahaye 135. Less than a year before war broke out, Delahaye began offering 6-cylinder engines with braking horsepower of 110, 120, or 136. BOTTOM LEFT: Sales of Delahaye's street cars, such as this 1938 Delahaye 135M pillarless saloon, soared following the successes of the company's racing cars. The conservative body was designed by coach builder Carlton.

to the car that could beat the speed records of the dreaded German racing machine at the 125-mile (200km) Linas-Montlhery Autodrome. The Germans often entered huge machines throughout Europe during the 1930s. Few competitors ever crossed the finish line first, and the French were eager to show their neighbor up.

Delahaye equipped its 135 with an overhead-valve 4.5-liter V12 engine with a twin magneto ignition and three camshafts with a braking horsepower of 200. Competing against Delahaye were the Bugatti, with a supercharged 4,500cc straight-eight engine, and the government-sponsored S.E.F.A.C. Famed French driver René Dreyfus was chosen to compete against the other cars, and broke the German record by hitting 146.6 kph (about 91 mph).

During the 1930s, Delahaye continued racing but never ignored its coachwork. Virtually every French coach builder had a crack at the Delahaye. Leading coach builders were Franay, Guilloie Pourtout, Saoutchik, Figoni et Falaschi, and Henri Capron.

But by 1939, World War II had begun, and Delahaye converted to truck production. After the war, it returned with a strong line of models, basically unchanged from the 1939 versions.

In 1948, the Type 175 debuted with a 4.5-liter engine, left-hand-drive, built-in radio, and Dubonnet front suspension. The car was offered on a 132-inch wheelbase with 140 horsepower for the limousines, and on a 155-inch wheelbase with 185 horsepower for the sports chassis models.

Delahaye continued offering a line of light-duty trucks through the early 1950s, but sales dropped dramatically as buyers abandoned individualized styling for the low-cost, mass-produced models on the market. In 1954, the company was absorbed by Hotchkiss, another French automaker. When Hotchkiss was acquired by the Brandt industrial company, it was renamed Hotchkiss-Brandt. The Delahaye badge was permanently retired.

RENÉ DREYFUS

French racing great René Dreyfus once recalled for automotive journalist Ken Purdy an amusing moment he experienced during his one-on-one battle with German racer Rudi Caracciola at the Grand Prix of Pau in 1938.

Dreyfus' Delahaye 159 with a V12 engine was pitted against the monster Mercedes-Benz W-154 driven by Caracciola. The Mercedes was heavily favored to win.

Early in the race, Caracciola took a healthy lead, but Dreyfus drove doggedly, and began pressing his opponent. As Dreyfus was driving, he noticed that his wife, Chouchou, positioned herself at the Station Hairpin. Near her was Caracciola's wife, Baby. With each lap, Dreyfus gauged his progress against Caracciola by Chouchou's and Baby's facial expressions. Baby was becoming more glum while his own wife was increasingly cheerful; the bemused and encouraged Dreyfus was indeed making progress. And when Caracciola was forced to make a pit stop for more fuel, Dreyfus sped by and crossed under the checkered flag.

Dreyfus was named champion of France that year. The Delahaye was only one of many racing cars he piloted during his sixteen-year career. He sat behind the wheels of Alfa Romeos, Bugattis, Talbot-Lagos, Ferraris, and Maseratis. His racing résumé is the envy of any driver: 35 victories, 19 places, and 17 shows. He completed 106 races out of 148 starts.

Born near Paris on May 6, 1905, Dreyfus began his driving career at the age of six, when he drove his pedal car, carrying his siblings and another youngster, into the Seine. His family limited his driving to bicycles for several years after that.

Dreyfus moved with his family to Nice in 1923, following his father's death. He joined his brother, Maurice, in the family fabrics business and decided that a car was necessary to sell their goods on the road. They bought a 750cc Mathis. Dreyfus tinkered with it to make it look like a race car and entered it in a race at Gattières, near Nice, in 1924. He won the race with Maurice at his side, but his Mathis was the only car in its class. One year later, he traded the Mathis for a Hotchkiss, and then purchased the true object of his desire—a Brescia Bugatti. Later, he found something even better, a 1,500cc supercharged Type 37A Bugatti.

For two straight seasons, Dreyfus tore up the road, winning fifty-five of sixty starts. He was typical of European racers of the day: polite, witty, and suave. Ken Purdy noted that while describing

With the city of Monaco serving as a dramatic backdrop, René Dreyfus, driving a Maserati, pursues another Maserati in the 1931 Monaco Grand Prix. Dreyfus spent two years with Maserati, and it was a very unhappy alliance. Dreyfus joined Maserati after being rebuffed by Ettore Bugatti. He signed with Maserati on the rebound, but his tenure with the team yielded few wins. Part of his problem was the continuing mechanical failures of his Maseratis, which forced him to spend too much time in the pits.

his experience at Pau, Dreyfus "talked about it with that air of urbane aloofness and detachment, habitual with him, that conceals his involvement."

Dreyfus was not an all-out driver who stamped the accelerator to the floor. He was calm, calculating, and precise.

He continued to win races at an amazing pace. Perhaps his greatest glory next to Pau was the 1930 Monaco Grand Prix.

Veteran Louis Chiron was leading a team of Bugattis, and Dreyfus entered his private Bugatti. The race was grueling from the beginning. Dreyfus' hands became raw, and were bleeding as the race wore on. But he held steady in the fifth and sixth spots and saw his endurance pay off as the Maseratis and Mercedes, among other second-ranked cars, dropped away.

About halfway through the race, Dreyfus found himself only two minutes behind Chiron. Next to his seat, Dreyfus had had a reserve fuel tank installed. His foresight was about to pay off.

Chiron stopped to refuel, which enabled Dreyfus to gain nearly a minute. He began stepping up the pace and flashed past Chiron with eleven laps to go. He crossed the finish line with a twenty-two-second lead over Chiron.

Dreyfus had hoped that Ettore Bugatti would find a place for him on his team after the victory. But he did not anticipate Bugatti's anger over a twenty-five-year-old novice beating the grand Bugattis in a private car.

A distraught Dreyfus went instead to Maserati, where his two-year alliance with the marque was unproductive. Dreyfus struggled with mechanical problems and bad luck, but he still managed to record some strong finishes, with second place at the Marne Grand Prix and third place at Rome.

At his request, Dreyfus was released from his contract with Maserati. The timing was lucky. Chiron had just left the Bugatti team, and Ettore Bugatti, whose desire to win races apparently was greater than his anger, sought out Dreyfus as a replacement. Dreyfus had a string of successes with the team.

By 1935, he was riding with the Alfa Romeo team, finishing twelve times out of thirteen starts. He won the Grand Prix at both Dieppe and Marne and took second place at Pau and Rome.

But Italy was taking a heavy beating because of sanctions from the League of Nations over its invasion of Ethiopia. Dreyfus thought that France was more favorable and jumped at the opportunity from Major Antony Lago to manage his Talbot-Lago team.

He remained with Lago only briefly before joining Ecurie Bleue, a private team managed and financed by Lucy O'Reilly

Schell, whose son, Harry Schell, would become a great Grand Prix driver. The team entered La Course du Million at Montlhéry in 1937, for a prize of 1 million francs (about $80,000 U.S.). Driving the same Delahaye that he would use to win at Pau the following year, he won handily against a Bugatti.

In 1940, the dark clouds of World War II rolled across France. By this time, Dreyfus was driving transport trucks for the French army. He was ordered to take a forty-five-day leave to accompany another driver, René LeBegue, to the United States to race at Indianapolis. Dreyfus and LeBegue did not perform well, but it was too late to return to France. Their country fell to the Germans, and Dreyfus was discharged from the army. He opened a French restaurant in New Jersey, but less than a year later joined the United States army. The Army at first refused to accept a French citizen, but relented after a campaign by Dreyfus. He participated in the North African and southern Italian invasions before returning to the United States to reopen his restaurant.

He later opened Le Chanteclair restaurant in Manhattan and stayed out of the racing spotlight. He returned on only two occasions. In 1952, he joined the Ferrari team at Le Mans, but remained in the race only four hours, when a broken clutch disabled his car. One year later, he raced with the Arnolt-Bristol team at Sebring to finish first, second, and fourth.

It would be his last race. He returned to his Manhattan restaurant and never looked back. Racing the finest collection of classic cars, Dreyfus was one of the last of a vanishing breed.

"Aggressiveness was not one of my major characteristics," René Dreyfus once said. "I would never be a Nuvolari." On and off the track, Dreyfus was a true gentleman. Never pushing his car all-out with the gas pedal to the floor, Dreyfus was calm, smooth, and very calculating when he raced.

After leaving Maserati, Dreyfus finally received his chance to race on the Bugatti team, joining fellow drivers Robert Benoist, Antonio Brivio, Tazio Nuvolari, and Jean-Pierre Wimille. He finished second at the Dieppe Grand Prix shown here, and later scored a pair of third place finishes at Monaco and Belgium.

Hispano-Suiza

LEGEND HAS IT THAT **C**HARLES **F**AROUX, CONSIDERED THE FATHER OF AUTOMOTIVE JOURNALISTS, WAS DETERMINED TO PROVE

that the quality of workmanship of the Hispano-Suiza was unmatched by any automobile in the world—even Rolls-Royce.

To introduce the automaker's new V12, Faroux drove without stopping from Paris to Nice, then back to Paris. At Paris, he

drove into a showroom and over a clean white sheet of paper where a small crowd waited for the

first drop of oil.

It never came.

Although the V12 was a complicated machine, Faroux had proved that thorough engineer-

ing, assembly, and inspection had created the perfect car.

Such stories about Hissos are common. One Hispano-Suiza owner reported that his 1921

model had more than 768,000 miles on it without a cylinder rebore.

During the first ten years of the classic car era, the Hispano-Suiza was the car of choice for

kings and princes, Hollywood film stars, and the nouveaux riche. While the Rolls-Royce captures

OPPOSITE: Extravagant by any measure, this 1933 Type 68 V12 Hispano-Suiza with a tulipwood body was hardly a practical traveling machine. The riveted tulip-wood planking was applied by the Nieuport aircraft company. Racing competitively was not this car's strong point, as it proved too cumbersome for mountain climbing and sharp curves. ABOVE: The famous flying stork on the Hispano-Suiza commemorated the squadron emblem of French flying ace Georges Guynemer, a friend of Hispano creator Marc Birkigt. Guynemer was killed in action during World War I in 1917.

most of the attention today as the premier classic car—probably because of its longevity—it came in a distant second to Hispano-Suiza during the twenties, when the rich and famous wanted to display their wealth.

Hispano-Suiza was the brainchild of designer Marc Birkigt, a Swiss national born in Geneva in 1878. Birkigt was approached by Spanish businessman Damien Mateu, who provided the financial backing to start building cars and to create Fabrica La Hispano-Suiza de Automobiles in 1904. Many early automobiles were manufactured in Barcelona, but later and grander versions were built at the Paris plant.

Birkigt first created two large 4-cylinder cars for the 1906 Paris Salon and by 1908 had added two big 6-cylinder models to his stable of cars. Production lagged those first few years, but Hispano-Suiza scored its first victory in the 1910 Coupe des Voiturettes. Hispano-Suiza then withdrew suddenly from competitive road racing. It was during this time that Birkigt developed what is believed to be the first supercharged automobile built in Europe. This supercharger had two extra pumping cylinders, but 1913 race regulations banned any form of forced induction. Birkigt shelved the project, and the supercharger was never tested.

But born from the Voiturettes victory was the Alfonso Type 15T, named after King Alfonso XIII, who had a great affection for the car. Powered by an early T-head 3,620cc engine that generated 64 braking horsepower at 2,300 rpm, the Alfonso was extremely light and had an excellent power/weight ratio. Birkigt combined the 3-speed gearbox and later installed a 4-speed one. Its top speed was about 75 mph (120kph), which was remarkable for the time.

Meanwhile, Birkigt opened an assembly plant in Paris and by 1914 had moved it to a larger factory in the Bois-Colombes, where the best luxury cars were produced in the 1920s and 1930s. The Barcelona plant continued to produce the more common versions of the Hispano-Suiza.

Like all automakers, Hispano-Suiza converted to military use during World War I, building more than 50,000 V8 aero engines for the Allied forces. In 1918, Hispano-Suiza began placing its famous flying stork on its cars' radiator caps. The flying stork mascot commemorated the squadron emblem of French air fighter Captain Georges Guynemer, a friend of Birkigt's who was killed in action in 1917; Guynemer's air squadron was powered by Hispano-Suiza.

Some models were carried over after the Armistice of 1918, but only a year later, the H6 debuted at the Paris Salon. The H6 was identified as either the Monza or the Boulogne and was based

OPPOSITE TOP: The 1912 Hispano-Suiza Alfonso, named after the King of Spain, came equipped with a 3620cc engine that provided 64 braking horsepower at 2,300 rpm. Top speed was about about 75 mph (120kph).
OPPOSITE BOTTOM: The Hispano-Suiza H6 chassis debuted at the Paris Salon in 1919, and has survived the following decades with enduring grace. This chassis still has a modern feel, with its excellent 4-wheel braking system and quick steering. The original H6 chassis Hispanos came equipped with a 6.5-liter engine that employed many of the engineering advances developed for aero-engines. The Hisso in this photo is a 1925 H6B.
ABOVE: The 8-liter Boulogne could reach speeds of up to 100 mph (160kph) and was in production for twelve years. It was known not only for its speed but also for its reliability. It traveled 580 miles (933km) from Paris to Nice in twelve hours, thirty-five minutes. In 1921 it captured the Boillot Cup at Boulogne, averaging 64 mph (103kph) over 237 miles (381km). The 1928 version clobbered a Stutz Blackhawk straight-eight in a twenty-four-hour speed contest at Indianapolis. In this photo is a 1928 Hispano-Suiza eight-liter Boulogne designed by J. Gurney Nutting.

on the aircraft engines that Birkigt built during the war. The 6.5-liter engine block was constructed of light alloy with 6 steel cylinder liners installed. It generated 135 braking horsepower at 3,000 rpm. It also featured four-wheel brakes long before Rolls-Royce did. The brake drums were designed to obtain maximum cooling with a finned outshell of aluminum over steel liners.

Many enthusiasts agree that the H6 matches most contemporary cars in handling and feel of the road. Such cars of the era, particularly those with long chassis, have a tendency to give drivers' biceps a workout. But the H6 had a light touch like no other car of the time.

The durable H6 remained in production in France until 1934. Europe's top coach builders were eager to dress the H6 chassis in its best metal finery, although the Nieuport aircraft company assembled an extravagant creation in 1924 by riveting tulip-wood planking for the coach. Andre Dubonnet raced this version that year in the Targa Florio road race in Sicily. The car had difficulty maneuvering the mountainous course, and Dubonnet was plagued with numerous blowouts, yet it finished in sixth place.

By 1929, Birkigt realized that his 6-cylinder cars were obsolete. His wartime experiences with the V8 had prepared him to make the transition to a larger engine. He created a V12 using the same cylinder-bore size of his V8 aero engines but developing a stroke of 100mm to provide at least a 9,424cc displacement. Birkigt abandoned the single overhead camshaft that operated directly on the vertical overhead valves, favored instead a pushrod and rocker valve gear. This provided a much quieter engine. The engine was finished by stove-enameling under pressure. With the exception of the Bugatti Royale, no other V12 engine came close in size and performance.

When one considers the bodies placed on Hisso's famous chassis having V12s, it is easy to recognize Hisso's threat to Rolls-Royce's reputation as the most luxurious car of the 1930s. Introducing the V12 enhanced Hisso's reputation in the luxury market, especially since Rolls-Royce did not replace its own 6-cylinder engine until the introduction of its V12 Phantom III in 1936.

The Type 68 was considered a magnificent car in its day, but it did not match the advances made by the H6 models. The car was only equipped with a 3-speed transmission, which made it difficult to crawl in heavy traffic. For such a big car—it had a 158-inch

wheelbase—there was not much passenger space. And although it could exceed 100 mph (160kph), it used a great deal of gas.

The V12 Hispano-Suiza remained in production until 1938, when it became apparent that war was inevitable in Europe. The Spanish Civil War had already broken out, and Birkigt was preparing for wartime production again. The V12 had an eight-year production run with few modifications.

By 1939, the Paris factory was producing only aircraft engines, and no more passenger cars were manufactured. In 1946, a front-wheel-drive V8 Hispano-Suiza was displayed at the Geneva Motor Show. No others were built, though, and the show car was broken up for parts in November 1958.

Marc Birkigt, whose sporty, lightweight luxury car was the symbol of the international crowd and set a standard for all other luxury car makers, died at the age of seventy-five in 1953.

Talbot-Lago

IDENTIFYING TALBOTS IS MIND-BOGGLING WHEN ONE ATTEMPTS TO TRACE THEIR GENEALOGICAL LINEAGE.

Between 1936 and 1958, Talbots leaving the Suresnes, France, plant were identified as Talbot-Lagos in France, Talbot-Darracqs in Belgium and Luxembourg, and Darracqs in England. And all this followed the demise of the Anglo-French combine of Sunbeam-Talbot-Darracq. But the car that earned Talbot a reputation for producing aggressive and stylish high-performance automobiles was the Talbot-Lago.

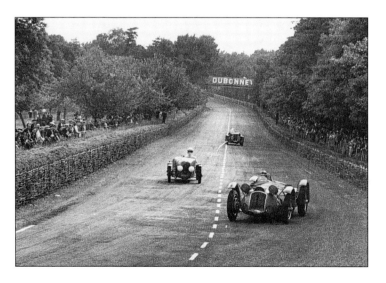

Major Antony Lago picked up the remnants of the dying Sunbeam-Talbot-Darracq in 1934. Indulging his overwhelming passion for racing, he developed a rugged, heavy car that had unmatched success on the racing circuit in the second half of the 1930s. The Talbot-Lago quickly emerged as a racing machine with a radical design, that is strikingly similar to that of many British sports roadsters of the 1950s.

Long before Lago came on the scene, though, Talbots had been tremendously successful in high-performance racing. At the 1930 Le Mans, Mercedes and the vaunted blower Bentleys waged a historic battle, with Mercedes eliminating one Bentley only to

OPPOSITE: In 1938, Antony Lago bored out the engines in his cars to 4.5 liters, allowing for 240 braking horsepower. A pair of Talbot-Lagos, similar to this 1939 Talbot-Lago Special, finished third and fourth at the 1939 French Grand Prix after Lago modified the engines to give 250 horsepower. Coach work on this car is by Figoni et Falaschi. ABOVE: A Talbot with its instantly recognizable high headlights is about to take a corner at the 1928 Le Mans.

find itself confronted by a pair of bigger Bentley Speed Sixes. But the most significant results were not the Speed Sixes' victories, but the third and fourth place finishes by two Talbot 90s. Trailing the Talbots were Alfa Romeo and a 5-liter Stutz.

The Talbot was very fast, required few repairs, and was as silent as a sleeping baby. Only this baby woke up with enough speed to send its competitors reeling.

Georges Roesch was largely responsible for the early victories of the Talbots, from the 14/45 that debuted in 1926 to the 110 of 1935. He focused on making every automobile devoid of noise, vibration, and excess weight, while at the same time demanding increased performance.

One of Roesch's greatest achievements was implementing high revs and high compression ratios in a small engine. In the 1920s, 5,000 rpm was considered top speed, but Roesch developed an engine that hit 6,000 rpm with a then-unheard-of compression ratio of 8.5 to 1.

He had his new engine tested at Brooklands, and it reached speeds of up to 90 mph (144kph). But the ride was so rough that the rattled Roesch became discouraged and dropped the project.

Out of this philosophy, though, emerged the 14/45 Talbot, which could hit 65 mph (104kph) with only a 1,666cc engine. The 6-cylinder engine was smaller, but the concept was the same. Roesch employed a very light valve gear to eliminate unnecessary weight from moving parts, thus creating an engine capable of high revs.

One thousand 14/45s were ordered to be manufactured based only on Roesch's drawings, and the prototype was not tested until shortly before its debut at the Olympia Show in 1926. It proved to be the hit of the show, and orders from customers immediately began to come pouring in.

In 1928, Roesch developed a much more powerful engine, which was interchangeable with the 14/45. The 75 series offered a 6-cylinder 2,276cc engine, which provided 93 braking horsepower with a 7 to 1 compression ratio.

Like the 14/45, the 75 had the radiator mounted on the cylin-

OPPOSITE: The 1930 Talbot "500 Mile" model, or the Talbot 90, had a 2276cc engine under the hood that provided 93 braking horsepower at 4500 rpm. This car is similar to the famous 1930 driven by the team of Brian Lewis and Earl How at the Brooklands. Lewis later raced on the Mountain Circuit with great success. ABOVE: Surprisingly cozy, the interior of the 1930 Talbot "500 Mile" model offered a very comfortable and quiet ride despite the rigors of the 1930 Le Mans. While the gauges are practically in the driver's face, they are easily accessible and comfortable to the eye.

der block with the radiator shutters fitted to keep the water temperature constant. This version, however, featured the first pressurized cooling system.

Roesch never regarded the 75 as a race car, but it was suggested to him that Talbot enter a team in the 1930 Double-Twelve (hours) race at Brooklands. He was eager to improve on the 75 and quickly developed the 90 series, which came close to achieving his original goal of producing an engine of very high revs.

The 90's engine had a compression ratio of 10 to 1, giving it 93 braking horsepower at 4,500 rpm and 90 at 5,000. The updraught Zenith carburetor was provided with a larger choke and jets. The 90 could run wide open for twenty-four-hours straight.

Although the Talbot team wrecked two cars at the Double Twelve, it placed third and fourth at the 1930 Le Mans, providing one of the most comfortable and quiet rides of any competitor on the road. The 90 ultimately took top honors in its class at the Ulster Tourist Trophy and the Irish Grand Prix.

Roesch then developed the 6-cylinder 3-liter 105 series touring car, which gave 105 braking horsepower at 4,500 rpm. The racing version provided 140 braking horsepower at 4,500 rpm, outperforming the more popular 2.3-liter straight-eight Type 35 Bugatti, which achieved 135 braking horsepower at 5,300 rpm. The 105 was produced between 1931 and 1937.

The 100 debuted in 1935 as a 3.5-liter version that developed 164 braking horsepower at 4,800 rpm. Its production run ended in 1939.

Up until 1935, Talbots were considered top-performing racing cars that had a number of worthwhile innovations. But little separated Talbot from equally innovative competitors. With races scheduled virtually every day in Europe during the twenties and thirties, there was ample opportunity for every marque to have a crack at first-place finishes.

When Antony Lago entered the picture, he transformed a good racing machine into a great one. Born in 1893 in Venice, Lago was equipped with an engineering degree when he entered the Italian army at the onset of World War I. He served with distinction, and after his discharge he immediately went to London, where he got his start in the automotive industry by selling Isotta-Fraschinis. That stint instilled in him the appreciation of fine workmanship, precision machining, and the detailed beauty of exquisite coach building.

Throughout the 1920s, Lago worked as an apprentice in the automotive industry. He spent some time with Lap Engineering of London, then joined the Wilson Company in 1925, where he helped perfect a self-changing gearbox. In 1927, he joined

Armstrong-Siddeley, and in 1932 joined its Alpine Trials team.

He was then hired by the Sunbeam-Talbot-Darracq combine and assigned to the English branch. By 1933, though, the Suresnes, France, branch was on the brink of failure, and Lago was given the task of returning it to its former glory.

When Lago went to Suresnes, the plant seemed like a patient on life support, but he saw an opportunity to put his own stamp on the automotive industry. He resigned his post at Sunbean-Talbot-Darracq and assumed control of Société Anonyme Darracq cum Automobiles Talbot.

Lago injected new life into the plant. Using the Talbot-Darracq 3-liter Type K78 as his foundation, he developed a magnificent car with chief engineer Walter Becchia.

Lago and Becchia created an inexpensive and efficient valve gear that used cross-pushrods of unequal length. The 6-cylinder, 4-liter engine developed 165 braking horsepower at 4,200 rpm and was placed on a tough, heavy chassis with independent front wheel suspension.

Here was an untested and unknown car coming out of a company that had been rescued from near demise. With the car's shaky credentials, Lago sought out racing great René Dreyfus, who was then with Ferrari in Italy. He persuaded Dreyfus to manage the team when his new car made its racing debut in June 1936.

Competitors were skeptical that Talbot could pull off a successful race, but respected Dreyfus' position at the helm. Indeed, Lago was not expecting any miracles, and actually agreed that it was unlikely the car would finish the French Grand Prix at Montlhery.

Taking Dreyfus aside on the day of the race, Lago said, "Your job will be to stay ahead of the Bugattis for as long as you can. That's all I want."

Dreyfus delivered.

The Talbot-Lagos clung tenaciously to the Bugattis for quite a while before developing various mechanical troubles. Yet all three finished the race, coming in eighth, ninth, and tenth places.

After that debut race, Talbot-Lagos captured first, second, third, and fifth at the French Grand Prix the following year. They also took first and second at the Ulster Tourist Trophy and achieved top honors at Marseilles and at the Tunis Grand Prix.

To save money and demonstrate to the industry that his cars were versatile, Lago developed a 4.5-liter engine that produced a whopping 240 braking horsepower and put it into a Grand Prix car. The car was flexible enough to allow for the addition or removal of fenders and other road equipment, permitting it to meet the varying

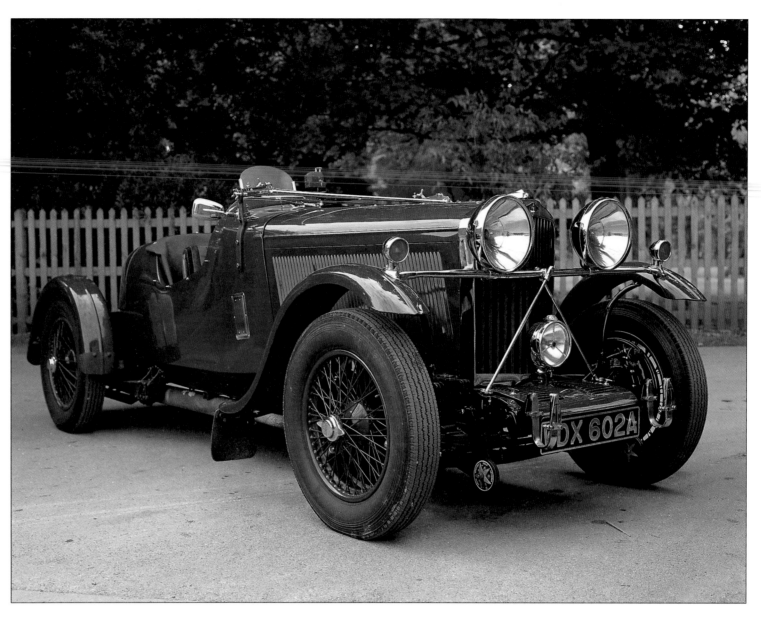

ABOVE: Veteran British race driver Rivers Fletcher described the Talbot 105 as one of his favorite racing cars. "Very quiet, like most Talbots, with great torque right through the rev range, real racing performance with uncanny smoothness and splendid handling," Fletcher once wrote. Above is a 1933 Talbot 105. OPPOSITE: A 1939 Talbot-Lago T150C.

racing requirements demanded in each event. This enabled Lago to race in both sports and Grand Prix events.

When Germany, France, and England went to war in 1939, Talbot-Lago shifted to producing aircraft engines exclusively. When France fell to the Germans the following year, production ceased completely.

Immediately after the war, Lago resumed production of the 4.5-liter engine. He also resumed his fantastic successes on the

track, taking first place in five Grand Prix races. From 1948 to 1950, Talbot-Lagos scored twenty-one first-place finishes in major racing events.

But in 1951, Talbot-Lago faced serious financial trouble. Production fell from 1,000 cars per year to under 100.

For several years, Lago raced with some success, but Simca took control of the assets of his small empire in 1959. Lago died just one year later, in 1960.

Part Four

Germany and Italy

Alfa Romeo

THE ALFA ROMEO WAS BORN FROM THE UNLIKELY ALLIANCE OF GIUSEPPE MEROSI AND VITTORIO JANO, TWO MEN OF DIFFERENT visions, who, except for a brief period in the mid-1920s, worked separately to make the Alfa Romeo one of the most respected touring cars of its day.

The car began exhibiting sports car characteristics as early as 1913, when Merosi designed a powerful 6.1-liter vehicle that sported 73 horsepower at 2,000 rpm, which was astounding for its day. Over a ten-year period, Merosi was largely responsible for designing and building the forerunners to the Jano-designed Alfa Romeos that became world-famous in road racing in the late 1920s and 1930s.

The Alfa Romeo was perhaps not as revered in automotive circles as was the Bugatti, nor did it possess the elaborate coachwork of a Duesenberg, but it is today considered one of the best sports cars ever built during the classic car era. With an emphasis on road handling and braking, it had what was necessary for top racing performance.

OPPOSITE: The 2900 B Alfas were originally designed for open-wheel racing, with a very light chassis and seating for two. By 1937, as shown in this 1937 2900 B convertible, appropriate street bodies were added for the public and the engine was detuned to a manageable 180 braking horsepower. Coachwork for these cars was performed by Touring and Pinin Farina. ABOVE: The 1932 Alfa Romeo 8C 2300 Le Mans was built purely as a racing machine for the sports car circuit. The engine in this model was very similar to the 6C 1750 series, but now employed two light-alloy cylinder blocks with dry steel liners and a dry sump lubrication system.

These overhead valves were operated by rockers and pushrods from twin camshafts high in the crankcase. Merosi dropped the engine into an existing 126-inch wheelbase chassis used for the old 4,084cc version. One chassis was fitted with Marco Ricotti's aerodynamic body and immediately struck 86 mph (137.6kph). In 1921, it was clocked at 91.6 mph (146.6kph) at the Brescia trials.

In 1914, the Grand Prix Alfa was developed for the French Grand Prix at Lyons, but the vehicle never made it to the race. World War I broke out, and the prototype went into storage. A year later, industrialist Nicola Romeo took over the company and the marque was renamed Alfa Romeo.

Many European automakers were impatient to produce cars in the months following World War I. But Alfa Romeo was slow to begin production, which did not resume until 1920 with the assembly of a few warmed-over 1914 models.

The 20-30 ES Sport introduced in 1921 was not much different on the surface, though it did offer electric lights and a starter. However, the area under the hood was entirely different: power was boosted from a prewar 49 horsepower to 67, thanks to a high compression ratio, a different valve time, and an increase in piston displacement. The ES helped forge Alfa Romeo's racing reputation as it swept through numerous Italian time trials, leaving many competitors in its wake.

Although the ES represented leap in achievement for Alfa Romeo, many of its components still held on to the prewar concept. Alfa management was eager to manufacture a true postwar model and also wanted a car that would serve as both a premier racing machine and a touring car. It found what it was looking for in the Merosi-designed Tipo RL series, a masterpiece in engineering artistry.

The RL had a 6-cylinder, 6.2-liter engine with pressurized oil supplied to four plain main bearings. The vertical valves were centered in a single file down the centerline of each cylinder. Like Bugatti, Merosi had idiosyncrasies that only a student of Alfa Romeo would understand and appreciate.

Each pushrod, for example, worked against a large and heavy coil spring in an apparent effort to avoid floating the valve gear. There was no automatic lubrication of the valve gear; instead, felt pads were installed under the rocker cover and were soaked with oil by hand—quite a job for the average owner.

The basic RL model was identified as the RLN and the sport model as the RLS. The RL was introduced in October 1921, but it did not go beyond the prototype stage until six were manufactured

ABOVE: The 20-30 ES was basically a warmed-over pre–World War I car that was first introduced in 1914 as the E 20-30. Different, though, were electric lights and a starter, and under the hood power was increased from 49 to 67 horsepower. This photograph shows a 20-30 ES ready for testing with the unusual Sankey artillery steel wheels. OPPOSITE: There is little doubt that Alfa Romeo, with cars such as this 1928 6C 1500 Sport, ruled the sports car circuit. An unusual feature of this model is the way the front springs pierce the front axle, while the rear axle is more conventional.

The Alfa Romeo's humble origins were in 1906 in Naples with the founding of the Società Anonima Italiana Darracq. After moving its operation to Milan a year later, the company went bankrupt in 1909. Its assets were acquired by a group of Milan businessmen who renamed the company Anonima Lombarda Fabbrica Automobili, hence the acronym ALFA.

Giuseppe Merosi joined the company that October as its technical director to design new cars and oversee production. Born in 1872 to a candlemaker, he had worked for the department of public thoroughfares in Italy before turning to automobiles. Merosi

worked briefly for Fiat in 1905. During the following year, he became head engineer for the Edoardo Bianachi Company of Milan, where he designed all Bianachi cars through 1909.

Merosi's first efforts for Alfa were the 4,084 cc and 2,413 cc models, which used an L-head valve layout design, abandoning the traditional T-head design still used by many American automakers. Although conventional in design, these machines established Alfa as a sound competitor in the European automotive market.

By 1912, Merosi had developed the 4-cylinder 6.1-liter version, which had two rows of vertical valves in its integral head.

OPPOSITE: The 1930 Alfa Romeo 6C 1750 was simply an enlargement of the basic 1500 engine. This was not done to increase horsepower, but to reduce stress on the engine and chassis and to give the driver more comfort. The 1750 can be identified by the sloping radiator, although some of the last 1500 SS models off the line also had the same radiator. This radiator was designed to allow for a supercharger mounted at the base of the front portion of the engine. ABOVE LEFT: While not particularly roomy by today's standards, the dashboard of the Alfa Romeo 6C 1750 provides an easy view of the gauges. ABOVE RIGHT: The cylinders in the 1750 engine were increased slightly from 62×82mm to 65×88mm. The engine was also available with a supercharger. This powerplant set the standard in Italian engine design for years to come.

in 1922. Regular production did not begin until 1923. The cars were very heavy—about 2 tons—but performed excellently in the factory racing campaigns.

Toward the end of 1923, Merosi produced the Targa Florio model, identified as RL TF, which was fitted on a light, short chassis and boasted 125 braking horsepower, a dramatic leap over the 56 offered in the initial RLs.

The RM, an offspring of the RL six, was introduced in late 1923 as well. It was a 2-liter, 4-cylinder affair assembled mostly from RL series components. It was retired in 1926.

During this period, Merosi developed the PI GP model, which was powered by a 6-cylinder, 2-liter twin cam similar to the Fiat GP 804. But the PI engine was severely lacking in power; even supercharging failed to boost its performance, and it was deemed a costly failure.

Merosi resigned in 1926. He later asked Alfa Romeo to reinstate him, but was rebuffed. He then worked as a consultant with Mathis of Strasbourg and later as chief designer for the Frera motorcycle company.

Suffering from severe financial woes in the 1940s, he eventually got a job with Alfa Romeo in its industrial vehicle division, where he achieved some success. In 1956, he died at the age of eighty-four.

Vittorio Jano was born in 1891 to a family whose men all excelled in the mechanical and engineering arts. In 1909, he began work as a draftsman for the Rapid automobile company; he joined Fiat two years later.

Fiat was then the undisputed king of the Italian automotive industry, and Jano led a comfortable life there. But his design ideas were not always accepted, and although he headed the design department, he was often treated like any other factory worker. By late 1923, he was being courted by Ferrari. But Alfa Romeo lured him away by nearly doubling his salary. Nicola Romeo was looking for a designer who would make Alfa Romeo one of the top Grand Prix competitors, and he believed that he had found that designer in Jano.

Jano served a brief stint with Merosi, working with him on the Targa Florio project and on a portion of the RL series. The two

men got along well and became good friends. Both men were methodical and thorough in their craft.

Jano's credentials were extensive. He had participated in the design of all postwar Fiats, which included every racing model. The best of the lot at Fiat was the Tipo 805, which produced more power per liter than any other car worldwide. It was a 1,979 cc straight-eight that used light steel cylinders with a ten-main bearing crankshaft. It had two overhead camshafts and was equipped with a supercharger. When Fiat introduced at the Tipo 805 at the Tours Grand Prix de l'ACF in July 1923, the car outpaced every competing racer in the field.

Based on his experience with the 805 and his keen knowledge of its weaknesses—the car was prone to excessive thermal distortion, among other difficulties—Jano designed the Tipo P2 for Alfa Romeo, which debuted at the Lyons GP de l'ACF in 1924. It incorporated the best of the 805 engine, and was a near-perfect specimen in every other engineering respect. Jano was determined not to repeat Fiat's mistakes.

Jano developed a manual regulation system for the spark advance, replacing the magneto system that had plagued the Fiat 805. He also found a way to vary the drive ratio for the supercharger by providing gears between the shaft and blower. With this modification, he was able to produce a small, faster-turning blower that created less heat and reduced auto-ignition problems of heat compression.

At Lyons, Alfa Romeo nosed to the starting line with the veterans of the Grand Prix circuit—Bugatti, Delage, Fiat, Miller, Sunbeam, and Schmidt. Alfa Romeo won easily, stunning its competitors. It won the circuit of Cremona, then captured the first two spots at the European Grand Prix at Spa. It would have taken top honors at the French GP, but driver Antonio Ascari was fatally injured in a crash while leading the race.

From the P2 came the 6C 1500 series, which sported the traditional 122-inch wheelbase chassis sitting on semi-elliptics and a tube-type drive. The 6-cylinder, 1,500 cc engine had five plain main bearings and a light alloy crankcase with a head that was detachable from the cast-iron block.

Production for the 6C series began in 1927. The car was considered more of a touring car than a sports car. During that year, six 114-inch wheelbase chassis were also produced both for a four-passenger and a sport model. These cars were manufactured through 1928, with a total of 150 four-passenger models and fifty sport versions built.

In early 1928, 157 cars were built for the second 6C 1500 series. At the end of the production run in 1929, Alfa Romeo manufactured 1,058 6Cs. The 1,750cc single-cam and twin-cam models followed, with some models having superchargers. Again, Alfa Romeo came out on top, winning three victories at Mille Miglia in Italy, a pair of twenty-four-hour Belgian races, the Grand Prix in Ireland and in Boulogne and another at Ulster. The 1750 series was built through 1933. A total of 1,865 cars and 714 bare chassis were manufactured in its five years of production.

Evolving from the 6C 1750 series was the 8C 2300, which was introduced in 1930. This was an 8-cylinder version of the 6C 1750. It had ten main bearings and many of the same components used in the 1750. It featured a dry sump lubrication system and two cylinder blocks made of light-alloy castings with dry steel liners. The crankshaft was made of two parts with two helical spurs between them. One gear drove the Roots blower located on the right side of the crankcase and another drove the camshafts. The 2300s took four first places at Le Mans between 1931 and 1934 and three top spots at Mille Miglia.

When the new 6C 2300 debuted in April 1934, its 2,309cc engine featured a twin-throat carburetor that allowed enough power to do away with supercharging. The ride was enhanced with the outboard mounting of the half-elliptic springs anchored in rubber. This time, with 95 braking horsepower, three Alfa Romeos sporting identical Touring Berlinetta bodies took the first three places at the twenty-four-hour Pescara run in 1934, resulting in the Pescara series of cars.

Alfa's first foray in the multicylinder market occurred with the 1936 release of its first V12. With a displacement of 4,064cc, it developed 370 braking horsepower at 5,800 rpm. It was equipped with a Roots blower driven from the front of the crankshaft.

Tazio Nuvolari guided it to first place in the Spanish GP, the Milan GP, and the Vanderbilt Cup on Long Island in October 1936. He also scored two second-place finishes that year..

Alfa Romeo's competitors must have faced these encounters with dread as the marque continued to sweep first place with regularity. The public, however, showed their approval of Alfa's success by flocking to the showroom to purchase detuned versions that had only slightly less power than the models raced by Nuvolari.

The 8C 2900 A also debuted in 1936, incorporating many of the features of the previously released P3 GP car. Like many of its predecessors, the 2900 swept the first three places at Mille Miglia that year. A street model was introduced in 1937 and 1938 as the

OPPOSITE: While the 8C 2900 A cars were true sports car competitors, the 2900 B was strictly for street purposes, and was designed with luxury bodies in mind. These later versions actually differed significantly from the 2900 A models, with the compression ratio reduced from 6.5 to 1 to a modest 5.75 to 1 and the weight growing nearly 700 pounds (315kg) more than the 2900 A. This car is a 1937 Alfa Romeo 2900 B convertible. ABOVE: Although the 2900 B never matched the speed and agility of its sister car, the 2900 A, it was still considered the fastest pre–World War II production car of its kind in the world. Carrozzeria Touring was the primary coach builder for the 2900 B.

8C 2900 B, detuned to 180 braking horsepower for the public highway. It was fitted with a dashboard, and coachwork was created by Touring and Pini Farina.

Although Alfa Romeo was acquiring first-place trophies throughout Europe with unprecedented success, its days were numbered. During much of the 1930s, Alfa turned its attention to aircraft engines. Jano headed the engineering department, but he was ill-equipped to handle the job. Meanwhile, automotive manufacturing continued to shrink. A mere ninety-one cars were built in 1935 and a dismal ten the following year. The year 1937 saw encouraging signs with 270 units built, but Jano foresaw the future and resigned, leaving the manufacture of aircraft engines to better qualified personnel.

Alfa Romeo's production was interrupted by World War II, then slowly began rebuilding when peace came. Alfa went on to achieve great success in automotive racing.

Isotta-Fraschini

AT ITS ZENITH, ISOTTA-FRASCHINI, DEFINED BY ITS ELEGANCE, PANACHE, AND PRECISION WORKMANSHIP, WAS COMPARABLE IN nearly every respect to Rolls-Royce and Hispano-Suiza.

Many Italian automakers fell by the wayside during the turbulent years preceding World War I, when various marques fought to find a niche in the market. Many of those manufacturers insisted that cheaper, mass-produced cars would enable them to remain in business. But there was only room for a few automakers, and Fiat grabbed most of the business.

Standing firm through all this hubbub, though, was Isotta-Fraschini, with its sound management philosophy and reluctance to capitulate to mass production. Even when the European motoring industry suffered through a severe crisis in 1907, as a large number of companies were vying for customers in a very small market, Isotta-Fraschini remained true to its strict design standards.

The company was founded by lawyer Cesare Isotta, brothers Oreste and Antonio Fraschini, and a number of financial backers to distribute Renault voiturettes, Mors cars, and Aster engines from France. Shortly after the founding of the company, these men began to import Renaults almost exclusively and then moved on to assemble foreign cars for Italy. The firm eventually graduated to importing French engines to be mounted on Isotta-Fraschini chassis. Not surprisingly, these cars bore a striking resemblance to

OPPOSITE: There is perhaps no luxury car that can be considered a greater symbol of aristocratic dignity than the 1933 Isotta-Fraschini Dual Cowl Phaeton.

Renaults, but before the French automakers could accuse it of plagiarism, Isotta-Fraschini began building cars of its own design.

While the first decade of the twentieth century was a difficult period for European automakers, Isotta-Fraschini, headquartered in Milan, benefited from having money and an excellent line of credit. The first true Isotta-Fraschini debuted in 1904 as a 24-horsepower, 4-cylinder T-head designed by Giuseppe Stefanini, who designed all the marque's cars between 1903 and 1905. He also developed two other models of 12 and 16 horsepower.

By this time, the company was reformed as Fabbrica Automobili Isotta Fraschini. Management brought in Giustino Cattaneo as its design engineer, who would remain in that position until 1933.

Cattaneo's task in 1905 was to design the company's first true racing car, the 120-horsepower Tipo D with an overhead cam, 4-cylinder engine. Three years later, Isotta-Fraschini was offering five models that offered state-of-the-art features such as a 4-speed transmission, multiplate clutches, and fixed wooden wheels. Oreste

Fraschini developed four-wheel braking, but this did not become standard until many years later. Two of the five models were equipped with shaft drive as standard, and the remaining vehicles were chain-driven.

Although Isotta-Fraschini was doing better financially than most automobile concerns during this time, it still needed capital to stay afloat. The company finally found a backer in Lorraine de Dietrich, a company that purchased half of Isotta's shares. De Dietrich also promised that it would purchase at least 500 chassis a year and produce cars designed by Isotta at its factories in Luneville and Marseilles.

The union enhanced Isotta's reputation on the racetrack, as it won a stunning series of races in 1907 and 1908. It captured numerous top honors in both Europe and the United States, but, ironically, this very success seemed to overshadow Lorraine de Dietrich's contributions altogether, a result that the French company grew to resent more and more. In 1908, Lorraine de Dietrich demanded that cars driven by Isotta drivers carry the de Dietrich name. Moreover, it was made known that Isotta management need not attend the award ceremonies.

These conditions did not go over well with Isotta. Less than two years later, the company severed its relationship with de Dietrich and managed to scrape up enough capital on its own to keep going.

The split with de Dietrich did not appear to hurt Isotta. In 1910, it developed another overhead-cam engine, which generated 100 horsepower and came with a unique water-cooled transmission, four-wheel brakes, and an enclosed chain drive. The car, a Tipo KM, offered four valves per cylinder and features that were clearly a result of cross-breeding with aero-engines designed by Cattaneo.

After World War I, Isotta-Fraschini directed its energies toward the elite luxury market, hitting its stride in 1921 when it debuted the Tipo. Designed by Cattaneo, the Tipo would remain Isotta's premier car until the early 1930s. Its engine was an overhead valve straight-eight (the first true production car with a straight-eight) with dual carburetors. Its bore and stroke measured 85 × 130mm with a displacement of 360 cubic inches, and it delivered 85 braking horsepower at 2,400 rpm. Later versions developed 450 cubic inches with the bore increased to 95mm.

With a 146-inch wheelbase, this underpowered vehicle was a monster to drive. Yet, though it failed to match the Rolls-Royce and Hispano-Suiza in performance, it proved wildly popular and was soon declared the symbol of aristocratic elegance. European and

ABOVE: The 1914 Tipo KM offered 4 valves per cylinder and other engineering elements often found on aero-engines. It had four-wheel brakes, a true rarity for 1914, and an enclosed drivetrain. OPPOSITE: A 1928 Tipo 8A Coupe.

This 1929 Tipo 8A was powered by a 7.4-liter engine that provided up to 120 horsepower at 2400 rpm. The 8A came equipped with larger tires, larger brake drums, and a much heavier frame to accommodate the massive coachwork.

American coach builders, gushing over the long wheelbase, conceived some of the most magnificent coaches ever assembled.

Many Isotta-Fraschinis were built to order, and a number of bodies were ordered by Isotta from Fleetwood, LeBaron, and other coach builders. Castagna and Sala in Milan were perhaps the most popular builders for Isotta.

And none of these chassis were cheap, even by preDepression standards. A bare Isotta chassis sold for $9,000. A limousine or town car body could cost more than $15,000.

Like its American competitors, Isotta knew the value of publicity, and continually attempted to find well-known personalities to link to its cars. Isotta dealers in New York often provided cars to actor Rudolph Valentino, who actually never got around to buying one. Ultimately, Isotta built a roadster for him, and Fleetwood was tagged to design the body. Aware that Valentino was an excellent mechanic, the designers gave this Isotta unusual fenders and a pair of running boards that ran the full length of each running board and were thick enough to support tool boxes. Valentino died before the

project was completed, but his death did not stop Isotta from displaying the car at the New York Salon in 1926.

By late 1924, about 400 Tipo 8s had been manufactured. The Tipo 8A was then released. This car's boosted horsepower of about 120 at 2,400 rpm could absorb the heavy coachwork.

The 8B was introduced in April 1931, and again the horsepower was increased, this time to about 160 at 3,000 rpm. But it failed to attract buyers; only about thirty had been sold by 1935.

The Tipo 8A Dual Cowl Phateon displays the elaborate coachwork of coach builder Castagna of Milan. Castagna was a favored designer for Isotta-Fraschini. But Castagna bodies and those of other European coach builders didn't fare well on Atlantic Ocean voyages for import to the United States. Often, Isotta-Fraschini buyers had American coach builders replace or extensively repair the bodies because of the extreme rattling and squeaks.

GOTTLIEB DAIMLER AND KARL BENZ

When one considers the origins of the automobile—at least on the American side of the Atlantic—Henry Ford and Detroit are usually foremost in one's mind.

Henry Ford changed the lives of virtually every living person with his mass-produced cars and the resulting vast network of highways and roads.

Consider, however, the efforts of Gottlieb Daimler and Karl Benz. As early as 1888, a passenger could disembark at the Stuttgart railway station and hail a motorized Daimler taxi for a short ride into town. And Bertha Benz tossed her two young boys into her husband's motorized carriage without telling him and went for a long drive, thus becoming the first woman to drive an automobile. With its emphasis on performance, comfort, and reliability, Karl Benz's second car, the Victoria, was the precursor to the luxury cars of the twenties and thirties.

Eleven years before Ford developed his first automobile, Daimler and Benz, unknown to each other, worked only 60 miles (96km) apart to invent the first automobiles almost simultaneously.

Daimler was nearly fifty years old when he produced his first motor car. Born into a middle-class family in Schorndorf, Germany, in 1834, he apprenticed for four years at a local gunsmith shop. The experience introduced him to the use of metal. He attended Stuttgart Polytechnic, graduating in 1859 with a degree in engineering.

Daimler went to work in England for Sir Joseph Whitworth, an armament builder supplying breechloading artillery for the Confederate army during the American Civil War. He pursued a number of engineering assignments before joining the Deutz Gas Motor Works (DGM) in 1872. Daimler, who became the company's chief engineer, joined forces with Wilhelm Maybach, the chief designer who would become a major influence in the original Mercedes-Benz.

DGM management quickly realized that it had a very strong team. Company founder Nikolaus August Otto had developed a four-cycle stationary gas engine. Daimler and Maybach improved on the engine, and DGM management sought to streamline production to boost sales. Daimler, however, sought to make his engines more efficient.

Carl Benz grew up poor and fatherless before serving an apprenticeship for a Stuttgart carriage builder. His first engine was a two-stroke version in 1877.

Gottlieb Daimler learned precision machining from a Schorndorf gunsmith who later sold weaponry to the Confederate Army during the U.S. Civil War. His first motor vehicle was a single-cylinder motorcycle.

Daimler resigned from DGM after ten years of service. Taking Maybach with him, Daimler spent a year developing a lightweight high-speed gasoline engine, which was patented on December 16, 1883. Less than two years later, Daimler's first motor vehicle, a single-cylinder motorcycle, debuted. Daimler's son, Paul, test-drove the motorcycle from Cannstatt to Unterturkheim with no problems.

The motorcycle set the stage for Daimler's first automobile, which would come in 1886. He ordered a custom-built carriage from Wimft & Son, a Stuttgart coach builder. The carriage was built to Daimler's specifications to accommodate a 1.5-horsepower,

single-cylinder belt-driven engine. Not only did Daimler invent a motor car, but Wimft & Son became the first automobile custom coach builder.

The altered twin-seat Victoria carriage carried an engine that transmitted its power to the rear wheels by different-sized belt pulleys. It was water-cooled with a unique finned radiator situated behind the seat.

Automobiles were Daimler's greatest interest, but he still found time to explore other uses for his gasoline engines. In 1887, he installed a 2-horsepower engine in a dirigible constructed by Karl Wolfert. The engine powered the propellers of the dirigible, and a successful 2 ½-mile voyage took place on August 12, 1888.

He went on to establish a shipyard to build and sell marine engines that ultimately powered ships for the German navy and harbor police.

Benz, born in 1844, had a difficult childhood. His father had died in a train accident, and his mother had to struggle alone to bring up her son. At an early age, Benz displayed an aptitude for mechanics and design. As a young adult, he began working for a Stuttgart carriage builder before designing a two-stroke gasoline engine in 1877. At about this time, he worked for Mannheim Gas Motor Works, but felt stifled there and founded his own company in 1883.

In 1885, he developed a four-stroke engine that would power his first motor car and exceed Daimler's creation by leaps and bounds. It was a single-cylinder engine that generated about ⅔ horsepower. The engine was mounted behind the seat, and the power to the rear wheels came from a pulley and belt-drive system to a true differential gear.

The complete car was not introduced to the public until July 1886. Benz had spent virtually every waking hour of the past year perfecting his machine. Benz's stationary engine business continued to prosper, which gave him the time and financial resources to continue developing motor cars. In 1886, he produced a new four-wheel car, the Victoria.

Benz intended that the Victoria be a fully equipped touring car with luxury appointments. It featured twin gas lamps for night driving, a horn, fold-down top, a plush upholstered seat, fenders, and an enclosed engine compartment. The engine had a float feed carburetor, a regulator to control the mixture fed into the cylinder, and poppet valves. The car averaged about 20 mph (32kph) and proved reliable for long distances. In 1894, the car was driven nearly 600 miles (960km) across Germany without incident.

Benz exceeded all his own expectations and those of Daimler as well. Daimler countered with his Phoenix in 1896. A new and improved Daimler Phoenix was prompted by Emil Jellinek, who demanded faster cars as sales tools for European buyers. It was not as luxurious as Benz's touring model, but it featured a 23-horsepower, 4-cylinder engine, which was mounted in front of the driver instead of the rear. This innovation eventually set the standard for engine placement. Thus, the Mercedes, named after Jellinek's daughter, was born.

Daimler died on March 6, 1900, and Benz on April 4, 1929. They led separate lives, but had the same philosophy of automotive engineering. It was not until 1926 that the Daimler and Benz companies finally merged to form the automotive empire that would produce the Mercedes-Benz. The legacy of these two automotive pioneers has become known for quality in automotive engineering and innovative design.

Gottlieb Daimler, in the rear seat, being driven in his first car, a carriage custom-built by Wimft & Son and powered by a 1.5-liter belt-driven engine. This photo was taken in 1890.

Carl Benz created this tillered, three-wheeled carriage in 1885. The single-cylinder engine was mounted behind the rear seat to power the rear wheels. It was displayed in public for the first time in July 1886.

Mercedes-Benz

NAMED AFTER A YOUNG GIRL BARELY OUT OF PIGTAILS, MERCEDES-BENZ WAS THE product of two German men who never met. The result of the genius of these men was an automobile of such superb workmanship that any German-built vehicle today automatically connotes excellence.

The crowning achievement of Mercedes-Benz was the debut of the 540K, which came during the height of the classic car era. Now considered one of the finest examples of automotive styling and performance, the 540K could reach 107 mph (171.2kph), and its body, constructed by the company-owned Sindelfingen coach builders, was unsurpassed by any other coach in the late 1930s.

Mercedes-Benz owes its success to the two men who were among the first to build automobiles. Karl Benz and Gottlieb Daimler were competitors in building gasoline engines in the 1880s. Benz, born in 1844 in Pfaffenrot, Germany, built his first car—a

OPPOSITE: The 1928 SSK had a shorter chassis than in previous years, and was powered by a 7.1-liter engine. In 1930 it captured top honors in the Grand Prix of Ireland and the European hill-climb championship. The SSK was similar to the SS model, but had a higher blower pressure for its supercharger, delivering 250 horsepower. ABOVE: Carl Benz displays his first creation, a tillered single-cylinder motor car built in 1885. The engine is mounted behind the seat. To Benz's left is his wife, Bertha.

The Model K debuted in 1926, the first year for the new firm of Mercedes-Benz. It was heavy, cost about ten thousand dollars, and was difficult to stop, especially when the driver pushed the accelerator to the floor, causing the compressor to kick in. In 1927 the Model K was greatly improved by its creator, Ferdinand Porsche. This is a 1927 Model K Cabriolet.

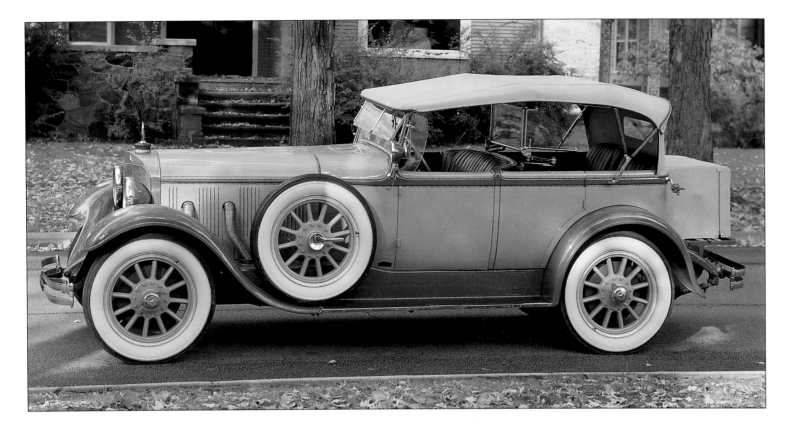

ABOVE: This Mercedes-Benz 38/250 SS, equipped with a compressor, carries a seven-liter engine with an impressive 7-to-1 compression ratio delivering 225 horsepower. The 38/250 SS went on to win the Ulster Tourist Trophy in 1929. The car was also a favorite with Lord Earl Howe of England, who raced it extensively in the late 1920s and early 1930s. LEFT: A 1930 Mercedes-Benz 38/250 SS badge with replica Sports body.

three-wheel affair with a top speed of 10 mph (16kph)—in the fall of 1885. Daimler, who was ten years Benz's senior, patented the water-cooled engineand was the inventor of the motorcycle and power boat. His first automobile debuted in the fall of 1886.

Benz, who formed Benz and Company in 1899, focused his energies on designing cars, and Daimler continued to build powerful engines. He formed the Daimler company in Stuttgart, where he produced powerplants for trolley cars, boats, fire engines, and trucks. Daimler later opened additional offices in Paris, New York, and London.

Emil Jellinek, an Austrian businessman, became intrigued with Daimler's cars when he witnessed a Daimler Phoenix take first place in a road race at Nice, France. Jellinek offered to buy thirty-six cars if Daimler designed a more powerful version of the

Phoenix. He also suggested—and Daimler agreed—that he name the new cars after Jellinek's daughter, Mercedes.

Daimler, who formed Daimler Motoren Gesellschaft (DMG) in 1890, never saw the first Mercedes automobile roll out of the factory. He died in 1900; the first Mercedes was produced a year later.

The Mercedes was unlike any other car on the road. It sat lower, and its wheels were set farther apart for better handling on curves. It had a then-novel four cylinders and four speeds, including reverse. It reached a top speed of 47 mph (75.2kph).

In less than a year, Mercedes was the best-selling automobile in the world. It began beating every competitor on the racing circuit. In 1904, it was timed at 97.2 mph (155.5kph) over a 1-kilometer (0.6mi) stretch and 109.6 mph (175.4kph) at Daytona Beach, Florida.

Benz, who believed that racing was undignified and dangerous, designed his automobiles as passenger cars for the motoring public. However, after witnessing Mercedes' continuing victories, publicity, and skyrocketing sales, Benz reluctantly decided to build his own race car. In 1908, his Grand Prix Benz debuted at the French Grand Prix. In what amounted to a standoff on the 477-mile (763.2km) course between the two German cars, Mercedes clipped Benz for first place.

During World War I, both Benz and DMG turned to war production and built high-quality aircraft engines. Germany's defeat, the resulting high inflation, and severely damaged factories prevented the two companies from introducing new automotive models until 1921.

By this time, Ferdinand Porsche, who was later to become the founder of Volkswagen, had joined DMG. He eventually became its chief engineer, and in this capacity he did revolutionary work on superchargers. The first production Mercedes debuted at the Berlin Motor Show of 1921. Two cars were displayed. One was equipped with a 1.5-liter engine, and the other with 2.6-liter engine, respectively, and both were supercharged.

While Benz concentrated on building trucks, DMG focused on sports cars. But by 1924, Benz was building sports cars again. During that year, Mercedes and Benz took home nearly 300 racing victories. Although these feats were impressive, times were hard as Germany was in extreme poverty. Many German automakers could barely survive, much less race new cars. Daimler and Benz were in the same situation, and in 1926 they merged to become Daimler-Benz. Unlike other automakers that were trying to stay solvent, the newly formed company did not slash prices and cheapen its product. The new Daimler-Benz, committed to its high standards, managed to survive anyway.

The K series (K for *kompressor*), designed by Porsche, attracted much attention. This 6-liter mammoth brute began in 1922 and was developed as a sports model on a shortened wheelbase. It roared with 110 horsepower—160 when the supercharger was engaged. It was the fastest touring car of its day and was the beginning of a successful line of other high-performance cars that enhanced Mercedes' racing reputation during Germany's lean years from the late 1920s through the early 1930s.

The K series was particularly popular in the United States and revered among the Hollywood film set. Actor Al Jolson bought three K series Mercedes. He gave one $21,000 version to his wife, dancer and actress Ruby Keeler, and another—priced at $28,000—to film executive Joe Schenck. Schenck's gift was a town car featuring extravagant gold-plated hardware.

Another K series was owned by Zeppo Marx. His Mercedes competed against a Duesenberg at Muroc Dry Lake in California and lost, primarily because of faulty spark plugs.

The K series was not a car for the casual driver; it could be downright dangerous in the wrong hands. It sported an unusually long locomotive boiler–type hood and was powered by the 6-liter engine that featured a single overhead camshaft driven from a vertical shaft at the rear. It had two valves per cylinder, operated by rockers. The crankcase and head were made of aluminum. The kompressor (supercharger) had a gear driven from the front of the crankshaft and ran at three times the engine speed, which cut in when the driver pushed the pedal to the floor. With the supercharger engaged, the engine howled angrily, sending horses and children scurrying from the roadway.

By 1929, the powerplant had been enlarged, first at 6.8 liters then to 7 liters. The 7-liter version, identified as the 38/250 or SS model, developed 170 horsepower alone and 225 when the supercharger was employed. An SSK version on a shortened chassis was lighter than the SS model and developed at least 250 horsepower when supercharged.

ABOVE: A virtual work of art that is considered by many automotive historians to be the near perfect machine, the 540K, such as this 1937 Roadster, was a wonder of suspension technology, with a complex radiator and a massive, heavy chassis. The 540K bucked the European trend of hiding the radiator by keeping it exposed as ornamentation. OPPOSITE: This 1937 540K special coupe is very similar to the 1936 version that stunned attendees at the Paris Salon de l'Automobile. The special coupe was believed to have been the first 540K displayed in public.

A racing version, the SSKL, came with a 7.1-liter displacement, generating a whopping 250 horsepower with the kompressor cut in. The SSKL was available to the general public, but it could never match factory road-test results. However, it was a formidable machine and performed well in many races. It won the Ulster Tourist Trophy in 1929, the Irish Grand Prix in 1930, and the 1931 Mille Miglia. Its best performance was driver Rudi Carraciola's 1931 effort at the German Grand Prix. With a lightened chassis—it was drilled full of holes to take off as much weight as possible—the automobile beat a pair of favored Bugattis.

Sprung from the original K series, the 500K debuted in 1932 and the 540K in 1936. Both were considered large compared to previous Mercedes offerings. These cars featured state-of-the-art independent coil-spring suspension and were powered by a 5.4-liter, pushrod-operated overhead-valve, in-line eight-cylinder engine. They generated 180 braking horsepower at 3,400 rpm with on-demand supercharging and 115 without it. The engine was

derived from the original 7.7-liter engine that was placed in the Grosser Mercedes, which was introduced in 1930.

The bare chassis weighed 4,000 pounds (1,800kg); with the completed coachwork, the car weighed in at a whopping 6,000 pounds (2,700kg). The chassis cost $7,000.

When the 540K arrived on the automotive scene, most automakers on both sides of the Atlantic had abandoned the external radiators and concealed them behind false grilles to enhance styling. But the 540K continued with the exposed radiator as its unusual ornamentation.

Coach builder Sindelfingen designed the 540K body and used the best leather, wood, and metal to build a palace on wheels. Eleven body styles were placed on the 540K chassis, including the two-door touring cars and a V-windshield roadster. Coachwork on the convertibles, however, proved to be difficult for American buyers, who had to wrestle with a padded top that refused to retract, ruining the gorgeous lines of the car.

The cabriolet was perhaps the most popular choice among customers, with 305 produced before the onslaught of World War II in 1939. Another popular model was the two-door sedan. Thirty-three were manufactured, and some were equipped with armor plating and bulletproof glass.

The instrument panel featured a tachometer, speedometer, oil pressure, water temperature and fuel gauges, and an electric clock. The 540K also provided a locking steering column, now a requirement on all U.S. cars.

Production of the 540K ended in 1939. It was the last of the production cars using superchargers. Mercedes continued with the Grosser model, very few of which were seen outside Germany. This largely ceremonial car, used by Adolf Hitler, toured the United States after the war.

With the war came the destruction of the Mercedes plant, putting an untimely end to the marque's specialized manufacturing and attention to precision building. Mercedes rebuilt its plant after the war and continued to produce cars of the highest quality, but despite its best efforts it could never match the attention it gave to the prewar 540Ks.

BIBLIOGRAPHY

Automobile Quarterly
    Vol. 2, No. 1, 1963

    Vol. 3, No. 2, 1964

    Vol. 3, No. 4, 1965

    Vol. 5, No. 3, 1967

    Vol. 5, No. 4, 1967

    Vol. 6, No. 1, 1967

    Vol. 10, No. 2, 1972

    Vol. 10, No. 3, 1972

    Vol. 11, No. 2, 1973

    Vol. 14, No. 2, 1976

    Vol. 23, No. 1, 1985

    Vol. 24, No. 1, 1986

    Vol. 24, No. 2, 1986

Automobile Quarterly's World of Cars. 1971.

Brazendale, Kevin, and Enrica Aceti, eds. *Classic Cars: Fifty Years of the World's Finest Automotive Design*. Exeter Books, 1976.

Carson, Richard Burns. *The Olympian Cars*. Knoft, 1976.

Culshaw, David, and Peter Harrobin. *The Complete Catalogue of British Cars*. William Morrow & Co., 1974.

Cutler, Robert, and Bob Fendell. *The Encyclopedia of Automobile Racing Greats*. Prentice Hall, 1973.

Georgano, G.N., ed. *The Encyclopedia of Motor Sport*. Viking Press, 1971.

Harding, Anthony, gen. ed. *Classic Cars in Profile*, vols. 1 and 2. Doubleday & Co., 1967.

Kimes, Beverly Rae, and Henry Austin Clark, Jr. *Standard Catalogue of American Cars, 1805–1942*. 1985.

Matteucci, Marco. *History of the Motor Car*. New English Library, Times Mirror, 1970.

Pfau, Hugo. *The Custom Body Era*. Castle Books, 1970.

Purdy, Ken W. *Motor Cars of the Golden Past*. Galahad Books, 1965.

Ralston, Marc. *Pierce-Arrow*. Tantiug Press, 1980.

Sedgwick, Michael. *Cars of the Thirties and Forties*. Beekman House, 1979.

Setright, L.J.K. *The Designers: Great Automobiles And The Men Who Made Them*. Follet Publishing Co., 1976.

Stein, Ralph. *The Treasury of the Automobile*. 1961.

PHOTO CREDITS

© **Dennis Adler:** pp. 17, 18, 19, 23, 25, 27 top, 31, 36, 39 bottom, 41, 45, 50, 59, 60, 63, 65, 68, 73 top, 82, 87 left, 94, 99, 101 top, 102, 109, 110, 113 bottom, 118, 124, 129, 142, 145, 148, 150, 153

Reprinted with the permission of the American Automobile Manufacturing Association: pp. 16, 44 left

Archive Photos: p. 69

Bettman Archive: pp. 22, 30, 44 right, 55, 66, 67, 111, 147 both, 149

© **Neill Bruce Motoring Photolibrary:** pp. 46, 51, 74, 76, 78 both, 79, 80, 81, 83, 85, 91, 96, 100, 101 bottom, 107 both, 115 bottom, 119, 120 top, 121, 130, 135, 151 bottom; **The Peter Roberts Collection:** pp. 84, 95, 106, 128, 134, 144; **The Midland Motor Museum, Bridgnorth:** pp. 98, 112, 122 left, 126, 127, 133; **Courtesy Brooks Auctioneers:** p. 108 bottom; **Car courtesy Terry Cohn:** pp. 87 right, 88, 89, 132, 138; **Car courtesy Nigel Dawes:** pp. 136, 137 both

© **David Hodges:** pp. 113 top, 116, 117 left, 125

The Hulton Deutsch Collection: p. 146 both

© **Dan Lyons:** pp. 28, 29, 33, 40, 53, 57, 71

© **Vincent Michael Manocchi:** pp. 1, 2, 7, 9, 10, 20, 32, 34, 37, 38, 39 top, 47, 52, 54, 56 both, 58, 92, 93, 103, 140, 152

Courtesy of the National Motor Museum: pp. 117 right, 143

Courtesy of the National Automotive History Collection, Detroit Public Library: pp. 14, 15, 49, 70

© **Quadrant House:** p. 115 top

© **Tony Stone/Photri, Inc.:** p. 104

© **Nicky Wright:** pp. 12, 21, 27 bottom, 35, 42, 48, 72, 73 bottom; **National Motor Museum:** pp. 26, 62, 64, 86, 90 both, 108, 114, 120 bottom, 122 right, 123, 139, 151 top